FATES

The Medea Notebooks

Ann Pedone

Starfish Wash-Up

Katherine Soniat

overflow of an unknown self: a song of songs

D. M. Spitzer

Etruscan Press

Etruscan Press
Wilkes University
84 West South Street
Wilkes-Barre, PA 18766
(570) 408-4546

www.etruscanpress.org

Published 2023 by Etruscan Press
Printed in the United States of America
Cover design by Carey Schwartzburt
Interior design and typesetting by Aaron Petrovitch
The text of this book is set in LTC Caslon Pro.

First Edition

17 18 19 20 5 4 3 2 1

Library of Congress Cataloguing-in-Publication Data

Names: Pedone, Ann. Medea notebooks. | Soniat, Katherine. Starfish wash-up. | Spitzer, D. M.,
1975- Overflow of an unknown self.
Title: Fates.
Description: First edition. | Wilkes-Barre, PA : Etruscan Press, 2023. |
    Includes bibliographical references. | Summary: "The Medea Notebooks by Ann Pedone: The
    Medea Notebooks opens up the ancient Greek story of Medea and Jason of the Argonauts
    by imagining three "Medeas": a re-working of the Medea character from the Euripides play,
    the writer of The Medea Notebooks herself, as well as the 20th century opera singer Maria
    Callas who played Medea both on stage, and in Pier Paolo Pasolini's 1969 film version of
    the myth. By weaving together three stories of marriage and murder, sex, and infidelity, the
    book seeks to explore and complicate our understanding of love, female sexual desire, and
    betrayal. Starfish Wash-up by Katherine Soniat: The writing of this ekphrastic collection
    began with the discovery of a 19th-century watercolor portrait of Telemachus kneeling by
    the Aegean seashore, back to his audience. Along with him, the reader searches the horizon
    for the Father (Odysseus) always it seems "off to another war" ...Telemachus thus becomes
    an archetypal symbol for the Lost Son, who really has no parental guidance (many times
    due to war). What remains across history is the many youth who in fact are still children
    of a missing parent. This focus repeats and circles into Modernity in this collection by also
    addressing the wreckage of our planet in current times due to Humankind's neglect-our
    own planet that offered us our first home. Life itself now in a tailspin in so many ecological

FATES

The Medea Notebooks

Ann Pedone

Starfish Wash-Up

Katherine Soniat

overflow of an unknown self: a song of songs

D. M. Spitzer

ways. Overflow of an Unknown Self : A Song of Songs by D. M. Spitzer: The erotic theme and imagery, along with its apparent secular tone, distinguish the Song of Songs (also known as the Song of Solomon) from the other books of the Bible. But whose love, which lovers, does the Song celebrate? Traditionally, the Song narrates the relationship(s) of heterosexual lovers, even as interpretations have offered other, allegorical configurations that depart from the heterosexual rubric. Translated primarily from the Song of Songs included in the ancient Jewish Hebrew-to-Greek translation project called the Septuagint, D. M. Spitzer's overflow of an unknown self: a song of songs opens the ancient poem to and for the trans-moment. By way of a queering translation practice that replaces the text's hetero-gendered pronouns with the intimacy of direct address and its I-you paradigm, overflow of an unknown self attempts to widen the Song's full-throated praise of embodied, human loving. Arrayed in eight "Cantos" that point back to the Septuagint's presentation of the Song of Songs, each section of overflow of an unknown self trans-figures the poem, diversifying the reverberant possibilities arising from a text always-already in translation. Hopefully this translation creates a zone where more numerous arrangements of loving bodies can imagine themselves in the Song's celebration. overflow of an unknown self works to fray and break the circle of heteronormativity towards an ever-expanding horizon of sexualities radiant with the bright, multicolored lights and possibilities of inclusion, of diversity, of love"-- Provided by publisher.
Identifiers: LCCN 2022013589 | ISBN 9781736494684 (paperback ; acid free paper)
Subjects: LCSH: American poetry--21st century. | LCGFT: Poetry.
Classification: LCC PS617 .F38 2023 | DDC 811/.608--dc23/eng/20220707
LC record available at https://lccn.loc.gov/2022013589

Please turn to the back of this book for a list of the sustaining funders of Etruscan Press.

This book is printed on recycled, acid-free paper.

Foreword

For our fourth Tribus, we present *Fates*, in which three poets—Ann Pedone, Katherine Soniat, and D. M. Spitzer—weave destinies by reimagining stories from the past.

Like the Moirai, these poets both foretell and provoke wonder:

what, I ask,
is the point of poetry
if it cannot make
even this happen.

~

Cursing in couplets, tweeting of human drift measured in masses:
poor continental wanderers—lost infants, men and women.

~

secrets lead my breath

       to you   where poems range

The books of *Fates* resist retellings. Instead, they reopen stories we have been carrying with us. They explore the limits and possibilities of form, testing the poetic line. And they invite new voices to *disturb the universe*.

Ann Pedone's *The Medea Notebooks* reimagines and reworks the ancient Greek story as three "Medeas": the character from the Euripides play, the 20th century opera singer Maria Callas (who played Medea on stage and in film), and the poet herself. In these lyric portrayals of marriage and murder, sex and infidelity, the book explores and complicates our understanding of love, female sexual desire, and betrayal.

Katherine Soniat's ekphrastic collection *Starfish Wash-Up* also claims a myth as its starting point— here in the form of a painting of Telemachus kneeling by the Aegean seashore—and along with that archetypal Lost Son and so many modern-day children, we search the horizon for our missing parent, a search that expands to include the wreckage of, and loss of, the very planet that offered us our first home.

Translated primarily from the *Song of Songs* included in the *Septuagint*, D. M. Spitzer's *overflow of an unknown self: a song of songs* performs an act of interpretive violence, shattering the heteronormative version of the *Song* and arraying its shards into eight cantos of trans-moments that ask us whose love, which *lovers*, the *Song* celebrates, while transfiguring the *Song's* full-throated praise of embodied, human love.

Each book of this Tribus, at once a daring translation and a rich original work of art, offers a distinct poetic voice. Yet, when read together, the books of *Fates* transform into a collective love song, three disparate poets all singing resolute, all singing luminous:

On this rocky shore
I vow to make for myself a new heart
One of mud and salt and blood
A cauldron of broken promises
And pale Greek lips.

~

Can I stick with my plans to temper hatred,
dress down slaughter, and find a tool rough enough
to scrape violence from the earth—its face and rosy

hindquarters?

~

I am an open mouth
of longing an omen   a hand
under my head another
slips around my waist

Make no mistake: this collective love song is devastating. But we surrender to the poems' terrible beauty, and the poets, sensing our devastation, liberate us by revealing how very much we belong to one another, and urge us to hear ourselves "beyond self/in the breath of another."

Etruscan Press

Table of Contents

iv. *finding time*

overflow of an unknown self: a song of songs   133
D. M. Spitzer

FATES

The Medea Notebooks

Ann Pedone

Starfish Wash-Up

Katherine Soniat

overflow of an unknown self: a song of songs

D. M. Spitzer

THE MEDEA NOTEBOOKS

Ann Pedone

"Love is much better, my dear, when you are not married."
                                                    —Maria Callas

Most books have one beginning; this one had three.
It began thirty-five years ago at Bard College when I had the
good fortune to study poetry with Robert Kelly, and the late
John Ashbery. It began nineteen years ago when I became
a mother for the first time. And it began three years ago
when a friend of mine got onto a ship in Athens and sailed
out to a small island in the middle of the Aegean Sea.

List of Characters

Medea
Jason of the Argonauts
The Writer of *The Medea Notebooks*
The Writer's College Roommate, Eleanor
The Writer's Husband, Jason
The Writer's Lover
Maria Callas
Aristotle Onassis

Medea's Prologue

I made of their flesh
no more than a sieve.
I had no idea what she
meant by this but
maybe it was
just a bad translation.
I looked at her and all
of the earth's matter
fell from her face.

Come,
let's count out all
the different ways
there are to enter
a woman's body.

Out Of The Mouth Of The Bosporus

I remember the sweet smell of the Peirene
that heady mix of freshly cut cyprus sweet
pear and bone on which I suckled as a child.

For the love of a man I traveled
over salt water dark as night
through the waves of Pontus' Gate
to live as an exile
a barbarian
in this land of Hellas.

Now with a husband
who has left our marriage bed in tatters
my body nothing but a watery hollow
thick with the scent of betrayal
darkened with salty mollusk
broken glass and blood
through which no man
will ever again choose to enter.

Language
flows
backward
up
through
this
fleshy
hole
between
my
thighs
into
a belly
now
emptied
of
all
of
its
milk.

The pomegranate seed
he placed in my hands that night
did not mean love, as I had thought.

iMessage

July 1, 2014 5:56 PM [The Writer of *The Medea Notebooks* and her husband, Jason]

W: You almost home?

H: No, still at the office.

W: Remember the reservation is at 8:30. Sophie is coming at 8 to watch the kids.

H: Text me the address, I'm probably going to have to meet you there.

W: What? I was really hoping we could go together.

H: Don't make a thing out of this. It's just dinner.

W: I'm not making a thing. It's impossible to make anything with you recently.

H: Ok, so maybe I should just quit my job and then I could stay home and take you out for dinner every night. And then you could pay the mortgage with your poetry.

W: Look, I'm not going to do this. You want to meet me there, fine.

H: Fine.

Patmos

There are experiences
that break us open
the body no longer contains
violence spills through flesh
this is the edge of myth
the Trojans are dead
civilization unravels itself
backwards
woman
becomes nothing more than
a metaphor
a system of ever revolving mirrors.

The days are foggy in Venice.
I've never been to Venice.

iMessage

W: Are you busy?

E: Sort of. What's going on?

W: I don't know.

E: Is it the kids?

W: No. It's Jason. I can't make sense of it.

E: Whatever it is, you should talk to him. Don't stew on it.

W: I can't. I don't want him to think I don't trust him.

E: You think he's up to something? You know how these guys are. They're afraid they drop the ball for five minutes and someone ten years younger is going to swoop in. It's the same with Doug.

W: I know. I'm probably just being paranoid.

E: Exactly. Don't let yourself go down that rabbit hole. Aren't you in the middle of a new project?

W: I am. But.

E: What?

W: I don't know.

E: Don't do this. You overthink everything.

W: You're right. You're always right.

E: Jason's not like that. Never has been.

W: I don't know. Just lately, it feels like I'm crashing into something. Or like something that shouldn't be visible, suddenly is.

E: Relax: Focus on your work. If Jason were up to something, Doug would have told me.

W: You're right. Fuck.

E: You want to go out for a drink tonight?

W: Sure. Maybe around 9?

E: That should work. I have to go pick up Ruth from swimming. I'll text you later, ok? But do me a favor. Don't do this to yourself.

W: I won't. Promise.

I.

She had gone downstairs
to turn the kitchen lights off
when she felt
the familiar press
of his lips
on the back of her neck.
I can still
remember what you
taste like down there.

A darkened kitchen at night
is a place where
Newton's Laws no
longer apply. The economy
of words and
the things they signify
breaks down.

This is marriage
as theater of sacrifice.
A race
to save what you can of yourself while
the house burns down around you.

The Greeks knew full well
that we are all born
in the bed of Aphrodite.
Trouble is, most of us
never figure out
a way to escape.

iMessage

July 17, 2014 8:43 PM [The Writer and her Husband]

H: Listen, something came up and I'm going to be home late.

W: Where are you going?

H: Down to the Rosewood. That guy I was telling you about, the one who works at Menlo Ventures. He just got back from Paris.

W: Ok, well.

H: He said they might have something opening up there.

W: Daisy's fever came back. I'm going to give her some more Tylenol.

H: I'm sure she's fine. We've been through this before with her.

W: I know.

H: What's wrong?

W: Nothing. I'm fine. Go do what you have to do.

H: Don't worry. But don't wait up.

Jason And The Princess of Cornith

My only crime
to open her legs like this.
My only crime
to taste of this
slow forming
hole in her sky.

I have surrendered
to this wound
to this thing
that gives
of its own light. Takes
of a man's beauty
and turns him
into a house of glass.

II.

But for love of the gods
what do you do
when you realize
you are a human being
in the middle of a mistake.

La Divina

Maria Callas was born on December 2, 1923
and was christened three years later at the
Archdiocesan Cathedral of the Holy Trinity
in Manhattan. Her mother had wanted a son.
It is said that after Maria was born
her mother refused to look at her for a week.
What happens to a woman, Maria would
often wonder, who is nothing but
a wound between her legs?

Naxos

No one told me
the rules for this.
One step and he's
in a hotel room
words
mouthed
under water
the taste
of her thick
on his tongue.

I won't talk
to you
of beauty.
She knows
he has a wife.

iMessage

July 22, 2014 9:44 AM [The Writer and her Husband]

H: You home?

W: What time did you get back last night?

H: Around 11. I was out with Tom. I told you about him. He was a year ahead of me at Stanford. He's at Kleiner Perkins now making a shit-load of money.

W: You didn't come to bed.

W: The party starts at 7:30. Are you going to meet us there?

H: You know, I don't think I'm going to make it. Turns out I have a business dinner. It'll probably go late.

W: Are you sure? The kids are going to be disappointed. And my parents are coming down from Sacramento.

H: Look, you know this is the busiest time of the year. I've got three deals that need to be closed, and that's not going to happen if I'm out at a birthday party.

W: Why is it always a choice between one thing and the other? I think you are the one who is making it this way, not them.

H: Look. I've got George on my ass all day, and now I have to take it from you?

W: Why was your ring in the medicine cabinet?

H: Fuck. It was pinching my finger again. I told you about that months ago. Why are you doing this?

W: Because I love you.

Ca' dell'Arte

Have you ever been to Venice
I have never been to Venice
but I know the smell
raw juice and dirt and cold plants.
Night comes and you try to find
a place to hide from the goats
you know will come out of the fields
and down into the canals
as soon as they
start to smell your blood.

iMessage

August 5, 2014 4:33 PM [The Writer and her Husband]

W: You at the office?

H: Why?

W: I just opened your Visa bill. Thought it was mine. There's a charge for The Four Seasons.

H: Maybe someone stole my card number.

W: Seems strange.

H: Jesus. If you're going to accuse me of something, then just fucking accuse me.

W: It doesn't have to be like this.

H: You make everything so fucking impossible.

W: I have to go. I need to pick up the kids. I can't be late.

Herodion of Patras

Maria Callas first played
the title role
in the French opera
Médée
in 1953.
Over the course of
the 1950s and into the
early 60s she
sang the part
a total of
15 times.
In 1959
she starred in the
Greek director Alexis
Minotis' production
at the Ancient
Theatre of Epidaurus.
In August
1960
it was reported
in the newspaper
The Kathimerini
that whenever
Callas performed
the role
in Athens
she always slept
with a knife
under her pillow.

Medea Somewhere on The Shores of The Aegean

What sort of container
Is a woman's body
This beehive this
Hornet's nest in which
I am held prisoner

Men leave their homes
Ripened for battle and glory
Roam free to civilize the world
Vanquishing monsters
Such as I

And yet we women live bound by the veil
Expected at marriage to be an uncut field
To live with our husbands as one flesh
Our own desires dissolved
In a mist of duty motherhood and sacrifice

On this rocky shore
I vow to make for myself a new heart
One of mud and salt and blood
A cauldron of broken promises
And pale Greek lips.

iMessage

August 3, 2014 1:56 AM [The Writer and her Husband]

W: You're fucking someone.

H: You have to put it that way?

W: Who is she?

H: No one. She's a vet. Her husband killed himself last summer. She needs me. She's like a project. You know how I love a project.

W: How old is this project?

H: Does it matter?

W: Of course it matters.

H: My lawyer is going to call you tomorrow. You can ask him.

Skorpios

In 1957
Maria Callas
met Aristotle
Onassis
at a masked ball in Venice.
A few weeks later
Onassis invited
Callas and her husband
Giovanni
Meneghini
to spend three weeks
with him and his wife
sailing the coast of Greece
and Turkey
on his yacht
The Christina. A month
after she returned
to New York,
while having
a late lunch
with a friend
at The Plaza,
Callas remarked,
when I was with him,
that man,
it was the first time in my life
I ever felt like a woman.

iMessage

August 4, 2014 4:21 PM [The Writer and Eleanor]

W: You are not going to believe this.

E: What?

W: It's Jason. He's moved out.

E: What?

W: He's been fucking someone.

E: Are you shitting me?

W: And here's the best part.

E: What?

W: She's 25.

E: Not possible.

W: All this time. It was right in front of my face.

E: What are you going to do?

W: I don't know. I need to find a way to pull these knives out of my eyes first.

Atherton

We live
in a strange hegira
where desire is
the only currency
where nothing
that is ours
ever seems spent.

And we are
ourselves
nothing more than
Bacchae
among electric lights.

III.

I cannot get over the sight
of her moving
toward him on her belly
the sway of her gold or silver it was
so dark in the room
I couldn't tell.

I watched as she looked
down at herself
while she fucked him
legs straddling his hips her tongue
long and dark noiseless everything
about her
clearly an animal
she saw me
in the doorway
looked at me and leaned
down over his chest so I could watch as he
sucked her breasts so I would know
he was in absolute
submission to her.

I can see why you think he betrayed me. What man would not
want to leave his wife for a woman with a hundred mouths.

Tragikós

In the summer of 1958
Onassis,
then married to Athina
Livanos
began an affair
with Maria Callas.
While the two would each
be divorced
within a year
they never married.

Callas never
mentioned
because
she did not
at the time
know
the word
betrayal.

iMessage

September 15, 2014 11:02 PM [The Writer and her Lover]

L: You up?

W: Barely.

L: I can still smell you on my fingers.

W: Get some rest. I know you're going to have a crazy day tomorrow.

L: Indeed. My first patient is at 7.

W: Then go get into bed. I'll be right here.

L: Sleep well.

W: You too.

A Lacanian Reading of Medea

Desire is such
a strange
mechanism
there are times
when it
works on you so
slowly that
before you know
what's hit you
you've been pulled into
the body
of another.
Some feat of linguistic
acrobatics
if you stop
to think about it.

iMessage

September 20, 2014 6:33 PM [The writer and Eleanor]

E: How're you doing? Sorry I haven't been in touch. But I've been thinking about you.

W: I'm good. Really.

E: You're amazing. I can't imagine having to go through something like this.

W: You're going to laugh but, I've started seeing someone.

E: What?

W: I know. I hardly believe it myself.

E: I have to pick Ruth up in a couple of minutes. But who is he?

W: You remember my friend Jessica? I was at her house for dinner. They had invited a few other people. And I got seated next to this guy. He's an old friend of Peter's from NYU.

E: And?

W: Well, and we started talking. I don't know. By the end of the night I was giving him my phone number. And two nights later we were at the Holiday Inn in Sunnyvale fucking like 16 year olds.

E: Holy shit.

W: He's really great.

E: Not another VC guy, I hope.

W: No. Are you kidding? He's a doctor at Stanford. Works crazy hours, is totally stressed out most of the time, but at least I don't have to listen to any more of that VC crap. And get this. He's from Greece. So when I told him that I'm working on a book about Medea, he got all excited.

E: I've got to go. You know how kids are when you're late. But shit. This is just the greatest news. Let's try to have lunch maybe next week and you can give me all the details.

W: I will. Ok. Go get her. I'll text you later.

36 Avenue Georges Mandel

On the day of JFK's funeral
Aristotle Onassis was with
Maria Callas at her apartment
in Paris. While the two
were watching
the procession, Onassis
suddenly turned to Maria and said,
That Jackie. There is something
Greek about her.

iMessage

September 21, 2014 11:33 AM [The Writer and her Lover]

L: Hi.

W: Hey there.

L: You're working?

W: Yeah. On the Medea thing.

L: Good. You know, in Greece all of our plays always had this thing called a χορός. I don't know how you say this in English. But I was thinking that all of these text messages you are incorporating are sort of the same thing.

W: Exactly. It's called a chorus. You're sure you're a doctor and not an English major?

L: Well, my head might be a doctor. But this thing down here in my pants is definitely an English major. And it's dying for you to take it out and suck it.

Poem Beginning "And"

1   And

2   The voice of Mary singing in the wilderness

3   Residue of Elektra

4   Creating out of the mouth of the dead

5   Paris

6   Paris again

7   Love me, that was all she had ever wanted to say

8   Drinking of the spring, the goats have no idea what is in store for them

9   She brought the prophet bread

10   On a raven-winged evening

11   Her body—explored, traveled over, circumscribed, exhausted

12   Marriage is wrathless

13   *Il y a un peu trop de femme*

14   The train passes. No one knows the destination

15   Do you take me as your lawful wedded wife?

16   I do

17   I do

18   I do

19   This is the aftermath

20   We both strike matches, in unison

21   Somehow, even in Paris, this goat-song is no longer convincing

22   Not even to the Greeks

23   Body trembling as over an hors d'oeuvre

24   And the dream ends

25   Spinoza

26   The goat is an offering

27   A prayer

28   *Τραγικός*

29   His heart is dry

30   Like the teeth of a dead camel

31   Marriage is a dream that knows no waking

32   Was it the sun you were looking for

33   These are the words, the song of a woman in love, an animal in heat

34   Now I kiss you, who could never sing Bach, who could never mend a sock

35   How wide my arms are
36   How strong
37   A myriad loves we will have
38   Myriad upon myriad shall be.

iMessage

October 1, 2014 1:23AM [The Writer and her Lover]

W: You up?

L: Barely.

W: Can't sleep.

L: How're the kids?

W: Good. You know, I don't think any of this came as a complete shock to them.

L: Still.

W: I keep thinking. What if writing all of this stuff about Medea is not such a smart idea. I mean, what if I get too close to it? Or it gets too close to me?

L: You planning on killing your kids to get back at Jason?

W: No. Of course not. But I mean, what if it all starts to play with my head?

L: Well, I think that's part of what writers deal with, right? Negotiating distance?

W: Right. But what about Flaubert?

L: What about him?

W: After he finished *Madame Bovary* he ran around France screaming, "Madame Bovary, c'est moi."

L: Sure, but didn't you also tell me he fucked little boys in Egypt?

W: Of course. But everyone did that back then. You're missing the point.

L: Look, go to sleep. It's all going to be fine. Just stay away from the knife drawer.

Medea's Decision, Part I

I am not Ophelia
nor was I meant to be
I will not swim
in a watery grave
I will force him
to see their blood
to feel it seep
into his flesh
until his eyes
have turned red

Maybe I was born
on the wrong side
of Zeus' shore
maybe my belly
now emptied
of its milk
leaves me
with no other choice

I will gather
the pieces
of my night
and cover my eyes
against the sun

And after my deed
is done

I will watch him
fall to his knees
But to whom
will he pray
for release
from this curse.

The American Hospital of Paris, Neuilly-sur-Seine

In 1968, Aristotle Onassis married Jackie
Kennedy. When Onassis told
Callas of the impending nuptials,
he said,
It's not love. I love you, I need Jackie.
The next night Callas wrote him a letter
explaining that if she could not be his wife
then she never wanted to see him again.
Four months after the wedding
he returned to Callas' apartment in
Paris and begged her to take him back.
After having rebuffed him several times
he threatened to crash his Mercedes
coupe into her front door.
Callas and Onassis' affair continued
until his death in 1975.

Medea Delivers A Short Lecture Before Killing Her Two Children. She's Just Come Back From A Week On The Island Of Paros.

a woman in pain
is a terrible thing
you can smell it
coming up
from between her legs
from a mile away

iMessage

October 4, 2014 1:23 PM [The Writer and her Lover]

W: Want to hear something funny?

L: Always

W: Yesterday my aunt and uncle came down for lunch. I must have left some of my Medea stuff out in the dining room. When I was washing the dishes, I heard my uncle go over to where the kids were. He started reading one of the poems out to them. The one where she stabs them.

L: What the fuck.

W: They all came running into the kitchen. Asked me if there was something I needed to tell them.

Medea Stabs Her Two Children Through The Heart

A wild god points
to her belly
and tells her
that she is bleeding.

I would suck the wound myself
if my mouth
weren't already filled
with my own sins.

Maria Callas' Goat Song

Betrayal can
start history
even a child
knows this
yet here
I am
a woman
prior
to history
music
prior
to words.

How
will my
body
continue
to absorb
the heat
of the sun
how will
these roots
feed.

iMessage

October 6, 2014 2:33 AM [The Writer and her Lover]

W: I just texted you something.

L: I can't believe she really does it.

W: It's crazy, I know.

L: But why?

W: Who knows. It's only with Euripides that we get her killing the kids. You don't find that in the original tellings of the myth. I guess Euripides wants us to think that for her, killing Jason would have been letting him off too easily.

L: Fuck.

W: I know.

L: Jesus. But doesn't it almost feel like he is turning her into a monster?

W: I don't think so. I think Euripides wants to take the lid off of marriage, you know?

L: Indeed.

W: I need to get into bed. I can barely keep my eyes open.

L: Ok. But before I go. Do a tired old Greek a favor?

W: Anything.

L: Take your panties off for me.

W: Let me turn the camera on first.

Medea After Having Stabbed Her Children

I have eaten them
drowned them
in this milky belly
from which
they once fed
my body now
nothing more than
glass words and naked
sentences.

Jason Confronts Medea

When searching for the lost, remember these three things:

1. There is no life
after death
certainly not for you.
You may scream
and climb
the walls of your night
but you will never
be allowed
to return
to a garden
green as this.

2. Newton tells us energy is neither
created nor destroyed.
I remember you in a field of poppies
yellow orange and sea-blue.
The wind in my face tasted of fig and
dark apple. You turned onto your back
and I watched as your thighs burned in the sun.
I will never again see
anything
as beautiful as that.

3. We soak our bodies in the oil of words
all our lives and yet now
after the thousands we have
spoken to each other
you are as strange to me
as the dark-eared goats
feeding on the grasses
beneath your feet.

Göreme

On October
19th, 1968 Maria
Callas agreed to
star in Pier
Paolo Pasolini's
film adaptation
of *Medea*. On
October 20th
Onassis married
Jackie
Kennedy on his
Private island
Skorpios.

After the
film
premiered
in Athens,
Aristotle
Onassis
arranged a
dinner party
on the steps
of The Parthenon
in Callas'
honor. When
asked what
he thought
of the film,
Onassis told
his guests that he
refused to see it.
How could I watch

that thing, he cried.
If I did,
I would have to
sleep with
one hand
on Maria,
and one on
my .45.

iMessage

November 29, 2014 1:33 AM [The Writer and her Lover]

L: You awake?

W: Not really.

L: The stuff on Onassis is great. That guy was such a little shit.

W: I know. Married Kennedy right under her nose.

L: And yet she stayed with him.

W: Exactly. You know, after Onassis died, her whole life fell apart. Died of a heart attack at 53.

L: I know. I remember watching on TV when her ashes were scattered into the Aegean.

W: Wow. That must have been something.

L: My mother loved her. Played those records to death when I was a kid.

W: I should get into bed. I'm starting to fade.

L: Go. Get some rest. You know where my hand is.

Five Short Lectures on Marriage, the Death of Her Children
at her own Hands, and the Loss of Her Youth, Delivered
by Medea while on a Ship Sailing from Athens to Mykonos.
In Front of Her She Can Almost Measure the Full Length
of the Aegean Sea.

The last crow
in the sky
has told me
that the light
of my womb
has been eclipsed
by my own hands.
I would say more
about this
but my mouth
is full of rotting
marigolds and green ash.

(penetrable
porous claustro
phobic
as a house of
spiders)

fuck me
from behind
like the half-
animal that I
have become

if only I could but fly
over this wide sea
as a man
then I would finally
be able
to eat the sun

what, I ask,
is the point of poetry
if it cannot make
even this happen.

iMessage

December 1, 2014 10:44 PM [The Writer and her Husband]

H: Is this a good time?

W: No, not really.

H: Wanted to check in.

W: You're going to pick the kids up this Saturday?

H: That's still the plan. But I'm possibly moving to LA. Within the next month.

W: For a job?

H: Yeah. I got an offer at a consulting firm down there.
It'll make seeing the kids a bit more difficult.

W: True. But if you choose to move down there, then you're just going to have to figure it out.

H: I heard you're seeing someone.

W: Who told you that?

H: Margot. I bumped into her at The Bay Club last weekend. We had a drink and she mentioned it.

W: Well, yeah. I am. Few months now.

H: Someone in The Valley?

W: Cardiologist at Stanford.

H: Oh.

W: Yeah. So you could say he is in "The Valley"-but not exactly part of your tribe.

H: Is it serious?

W: Possibly. How's what's-her-name?

H: Liz? She went back to Madison two months ago. Found a job at a clinic there.

W: She didn't ask you to go with her?

H: Follow a 25 year old to Wisconsin?

W: Well, sorry.

H: Thanks.

W: Wait, no, actually, fuck sorry.

H: I'll get the kids on Saturday.

IV.

If we understood
how the moon
gets its light
so far down
that it is here
under this bracken
between
my toes
swimming
through these leaves
then maybe we could
begin to
comprehend
the end of
a woman's life.

The holes of my body
have all closed tight
all that is left
is for me to eat
myself alive.

iMessage

November 18, 2014 2:31AM [The Writer and her Lover]

L: You up?

W: Can't sleep.

L: I just finished reading what you sent this morning. Even when you know it's coming, it's still hard to believe.

W: I know. She wanted to get back at Jason, but ends up burning the whole house down.

L: This is what I've been trying to tell you. I don't care what anybody says, the ancient Greeks were totally fucked.

STARFISH WASH-UP

Katherine Soniat

For Celine, and Shelton and Ashton

I would wish, my son, that your love for me were less tender and more manly; you must learn to bear my absence, said Mentor who then inspired in Telemachus virtues that are seldom found united: intrepid valor and calm moderation.

—Mentor's words to Telemachus from *The Adventures of Telemachus Odysseus's Son* by Francois de la Mothe Fenelon 1776
(translation: Tobias Smollett)

Manuscript notes:

Sanskara: Within Hindi tradition, *sanskara* translates to "he who flows into himself" and thus becomes the perpetual wanderer passing through previous time—one's same illusion of self, again and again.

Starfish Wash-up is best read sequentially within each section. . . and also from section to section, as one reads a novel. This approach allows for a dissolving context in which time and space blur—only to reassemble in as part of the vaguely familiar. Such pattern enables archetype (here, of the lost children of wars, and also that which environmentally is ignored/or uncared for by *mankind*) to play an integral role in the sequential arrangement of this manuscript.

i. *after birth*

Telemachus Seeking

At war, the present-tense of our world—bodies marched off two legs
at a time.   Swine, lambs, heifers and lovers rolled up as one and fed

as slaughter.   *Leave at once, you greedy scoundrels:* wail of those long ago
obscured and deleted near the Aegean.

~

Telemachus kneels on the shore, the gray waves breaking. He scans
the horizon for his father. If not by the sea spread before him, he's

baffled by the hypnosis of looking—home changed to a vaulted
museum of men baying for mothers.

~

Calm then wild, the sea confounds. Where but the shoreline can a ghost
and his son be familiar?

The constancy of lost Odysseus—he and Telemachus as if they were roped
together in foam.   They share the ocean-keeper's eyes.

~

Supplicant at the missing fathers' feet.   Sons beg for a guardian
not departure.   But it's a child's guess as who actually crosses

the threshold.   Either way, the doorway fills then empties.
No lit gods cure Telemachus, hoping.   History's bloodied

adore endless battle—those   the never-banned idols of men.
Ghost-makers all.

~

Burst of thunder   as from wide and far the Greeks gather.   Farther
away   Odysseus sails.

Telemachus imagines boats and men   that come to nothing. Shipwreck
of stars in the sky at dark.   Phantoms pay homage to nothing.

                        ~

This boy's *Bring My Lord Home* song twists the mind.   Chant
of sons that need more.   He cannot stop his father-husband men

from arriving at night (one for Penelope too). Thoughts swim
inside him but not a soul stops to think   that such wishing

never will do.   Stories of home tell us so.

Penelope's Womb

Telemachus glides about the dream-table of fresh bowls of milk.
Mother and father look at him   then to each other. Nurse
smiles from the womb   currant tarts warm in her apron
so boy first will know sweetness.

What brilliant shocks wait for the newborn.

~

Telemachus (grown taller now) sits in a sea-cave
with the gulls   to figure his own charging body.

He touches new hairs down past his belly—golden
braille continent of fathers leaving.

Taken by the sea   Odysseus sailed   blew   then flew
into the arms of Circe—enchanter attached to the heart.

Lure for men to leave wives, daughters and mothers.
House-of-cards son running (to and away from) home:
Penelope with her would-be lovers.

~

Islands blow from the ocean floor.   Wars glisten.

Our shattered lineage.

Losing Touch

i. *Him*

at war on the Pacific. Always that ocean. Swine, lamb, heifers
and lovers rolled up as one, and fed as garbage.

No more family near the Washington Zoo. My father abounds
where it's tidal, and for decades thereafter I sense him springing

about—bombers headed for his hot metal deck of munitions.

ii. *To hell*

he screams back at the war when he comes home to curse
and drink. Drunk, he does not want to go where the big green

vases fly in a westerly direction . . . those he hurled at sunset.
When the bureau collapses into the hallway, he can't back away

fast enough. Stuck to his ship most nights, he's an ocean
on fire.

iii. *My twilight*

house reels with the *up, down and jump now*
commands to the living. Screams. Lungs raw. Flesh

of men overboard.   Those paralytic times repeat
like paleontology: Neither bones nor the failed human heart

can be better behaved.   To [be able to] do anything at that
point in time. . . the sheer magnitude of roll over, and die again.

iv. *You*

Your hands go down   then up over your head in the bathroom.
Lukewarm plunges from the tub faucet behind you.   That heard,

you surrender.   Water stupefies.   Medicine-chest mirror
with water running wildly through you . . . the shock of catching

yourself time-lapse in a mirror— another cracked, crooked-faced
soul on its feet.

v. *Adrenalin*

rushes are worth other wars . . . you storming
the kitchen as if best friend to a hungry sea of animals.

Walls and ceiling loudly   tilt.   Ready to drown,
I am the part that can't find   land.   *Won't you, please,*

go away, with all those flames wiggling wetly around you.

vi. *Family*

trees   for those who patiently wait to be born.   My
chance at daughter.   Mouthful of devils I keep handy.

Little spit-fire, you yell.   Thoroughly informed
I turn loose   as lions in cages roar along

with so many people from so much time   scurrying across the earth:
just not to be lugged away   shoved under   or forgotten.

vii. *Humans*

clipped away by the great cosmic fan.   Flesh in fiery blue garb
streaks inside my planetary doom.   *Dome,* I mean, that yellow

bedroom ceiling.   My kitchen   zoo   and bathroom
crazy for peace.

I pick the past from your eyes.   It makes me snap my teeth—one,
two, three—to hold you at a distance.   Not believing in the possibilities

of water, you explode   and I need something solid to live on.

viii. *Creatures*

of war learn hate early.   My job is to seal gold paper
walls.   The voice says, *Play you're alive. Open your mouth wide*

but don't make a sound.   I'm mostly feeling the whales and how
their guts must be hurting.   You think about this one with me.

But still there's this woman we have between us . . .
the mother/wife who cannot leave us alone

ix. *Strength*

I don't have the strength to get us all up off the floor at once—
mass of melted bourbon mixing with your Pacific.

Any way terror is absorbed what matters most is how
(quickly) a body stands up.   Then to get back

to the prehistory of *quietly.*   And *delicate.*
Or at least to have records, annals of the muddled,

broken soldiers.   The sheepish and mute.
          Our most secret garden.

x.   *Kwan Yin Waiting*

Mothers seem less visible at the end   or more

visibly convoluted   In my family we had a total of six
arms   with muscles   and three heads—one made for only a child

Those parts were intact . . . unlike my brush with Kwan Yin

the goddess of compassion who rides her foamy dragons
across a dark China Sea.

Cross the water, she points a way to me.

Then too [and mainly with her eyes] she warns
Mercy to a world in misery.

Kwan Yin stands above the ragged   ripped   and soul-dead
as they cry   *water   touch   Look at me*

and she offers a literal translation
*to live without | and inside the flesh | and from the heart
and never ever to stop*

Even as the mind launches its fireball of *Mine-
mine-it's-all-mine-so-give-it-here-or-I'll-skin-you alive.*

Island

My son cares for his own first home,
hammering. Raking and watering. Like some

kind of father, I think sleepily listening to the gulf.
These sounds of domesticity bring back my husband

the first year we were married.   The word *father* fractures and
the one who manifests in dream is mine: My father leans,

a face so close—his smile and eyes whimsical as if we'd shared
the same secret for decades. Something laughable holds us

a kiss-length apart . . . this man who wobbled feet-first out of war
then surrounded himself with water.

Afterthought

For seasons by the water, then finally knowing what's missing,
            Telemachus gets it.
Gotten, he puts away yearning. His mission of hoping.

No more days eaten up by men or their ships.

(be sure death not your first thought of the day
or choice.)

Succumb to the present—even when it's an estranged
dwelling of suitors.

Who cares about me, a mishap sorrow near the water?

The horizon long and thin,
                              stretches.   Kneeling
this long in the sand guarantees my hole
will be even deeper.

Telemachus Ponders the Bottomland

How might I return to the land named after brightness,
the home where lit mice once ran the fields
and thrived on barley?

And who thought up lines this sharply pointed:
      Drink only from that fountain. Leave your skin at the door.
Broken animal ribs served at cliff bottom. Bottomland pox on those
who love the wrong gender.
               Don't those phrases, no matter how dated,
sound like the way we humans think?   How a swift
jolt of war makes us as wicked as any—even those who wished they had
done what others had   And they kept on wishing
for an awful long time.

The Magical Age of Quitting

But please let's return to my perfect outrage:
how can some duplicitous voice then warn
me, *do be careful where you travel*
after birth?

Entanglements drag us through time.
Foreshadow.   Post-shadow,
or preemptive strikes of magic

matter not at all

for I did it. . . it was me/Telemachus
who was born and took on that status as trophy

sacks of grain for rats to eat in winter.

That Morning I Saw Telemachus

painted on a page in the book,
his back was to me.

I was not close.

Even then   I knew he was apex and text with plans
bigger than death.

Dream child.   Frozen ballet of the water-boy who counts
on the right ship coming home—but never gets the one ordered.

This boy does not turn to me.

His posture is stoic.

Perhaps   my absence served him.   Departure
is why I am called to this reckoning.

Telemachus's song was mine too as a child: *Lord (and Lady)*
are you ever coming home?   *and when?*

Gaze into darkness beyond my window

I am trying to hookup in the waves
or pass under

A blessing was I for him learning to speak
for and to himself   More than sound

crosses the water

Floating Encampments

Life loops about only to thicken in the womb—
then to walk the beach as a later spot
slowly changing to boy.

Perhaps that's why Telemachus was an erratic child—
dizzily conceived   and trained in mid-sand
to doubt the eternal nature   of fathers.

Is the brain of a child born hesitating?

Signal fires burn on coastal islands: men in waiting
for bedlam.

Floating encampments.

Was there ever a homegrown embryo
in some woman's belly—outline and shadow
set quietly inside her?

After Birth

When
the baby finally
arrives   vinegar
and white hibiscus
pour through the clouds
as once her undergarments
fell from the bed and on hands
and knees she crawled to fish the
flimsiest forward—she the first to
know their movement and departure.
Sprinkled rosewater on a new moon

ii. *first nature*

Half Life

In her perfumed dream, golden cords
open the curtain on fox.

Under a green crown of fern, he is barking.

As feral a cry you'll not hear than this red beast
struggling.

The orchestrated humans fall silent by dawn.

Sepia   those half-lives in the apricot trees.
First cousin this hour is to my old collection of lace,

the ever ghosts.

Throats puffed open.   Lung hung mammalian
under the morning star.

At Large

The winged-warrior pathologies
antiquely arranged are meant to stay.   Why blame old cartographer
for plans on water?   Or latter-day men who came
to want more and more of the land—scratching Earth hard
after wealth? After-wars.

So what if separations (of fiefdoms, dynasties, and the family pigs)
become an elephantine question?

It's that large and clumsy—our uncomfortably wrinkled guest
on the sleeping porch, all over the west wing, and great hall
of leaky red meats.

However you describe it, the big bones are anticipate
as we suck grease from our fingers, then yell for more.

Missing Parts

Recall where the idea of you (or me) came from
in the first place? Man and woman on a tear with scrolls
in four hands: giant plans on how to improve one another.

Indeed, my two waited breathlessly by the Aegean until
I shuddered forth from Penelope's womb.

Slowly they disappeared.　　　　　　　And because few
answered for much in my day, and nothing belonged to my
mother　　　　　　naturally there was little accounting.

Was it one or both of them who went missing, and does that matter?
Who's to say who felt the most-worst about leaving. Active or passive,

it's a homeless journey.

Greed

What to make of the acquisitive mind,
bloating?
          Maybe just delete that plush interior
before it includes us in its most secret plans.

Look at that soup bowl   how an empty concave
needs for more at a glance.

Was *I* the first mark of selfishness ever?

Can I stick with my plans to temper hatred,
dress down slaughter, and find a tool rough enough
to scrape violence from the earth—its face and rosy

hindquarters?

Agua

Childlike ones don't tattle on the choice of stepfathers.
Compendiums of quiet they are—the bathtub girls
remain hushed   and become legends in waiting.

Something happened to my medicine-cabinet mirror
as it began to shake and would not stop,

which is consistent with the story nobody knows.

Silence simmers like butter   oddly
(and goldenly) brought to froth but never does it
clarify into language.

My father-man's face   I caught glimpses of—
that man always would be in my keeping.

More phantom (than not)
he breathed from that bathroom mirror.

A spotty history   no man wants to own.
Invincible.   Never-heart of the canyon.

For sure it is her/me   his naked prey in the tub
Underwater refractions.   Blue/green.

He watches me spot him in glass.

With such aquatic vision, time should have been mine.
My space in which to ask, *Whose bath comes dripping*

in dreams with that same clear-glass girl

up to her neck in water?

Violet

In her dream of cherry trees
is winter

Frozen   she was :   : thoughts like that offered weight
to her being

Out of all those branches there should have be one strong enough
to hold a swing full of her
                              up and out there   and never
to break

Numb she felt as any child who sees men with glass eyes
   in every mirror

Orphan Joy

Send Kwan Yin home to me   her messages of compassion pressed
between book covers   Mail her to the wrought-iron

number nine nailed to my cottage where geese stay all winter
No more measured words are written   Your silence

is measurable   a cowardly and inept voice on the planet   *Wait*
spilt in blue across my open palm   Kwan Yin walked

the tracks with me   the lake never far   Geese die—
      shot in both wings   Nothing else

Comfort Food

How can children with parents wash up on the beach
(spread out in lines) grow sadder and stiffer before you
on TV?

Your eyes have seen this.   They have.
Think *this too will pass?*   No luck, my friend:

Bloodied lambs, the busted granary workers, pheasants
nailed to the barn wall.   Look them in each glazed eye
and say   *You were part of our fancy passing.   A fad.*

Remarkably too, those episodes of hiding in trees
to kill animals that have us feel strong and well-fed
before bed.

At home, we are with killing—our radical home-
sickness.

Scream

gordian one at those who hesitate and will not
come undone,　　　　or ever go away.

I place my knee to press Telemachus's young spine
up by the sea.

He has few answers for the waves.

What else is there for him to do. . . but hang upside down
and fetal in a glass bottle of lost ships?

Children feel what absence means.

Words drift up sideways then sink into the Eight Ball
of Childhood where for one inky instant the alphabet coheres
with *yes indeed,*　　then slips untenably into: *come back later*
(if you're around in some other life).

First Nature, Once Removed

Is childhood different from any body of (loose) clothing or rising water? Make
of it what you will.   I did.   Some are grounded by target practice

but return with leaks known as homesickness for life.   Wobbly
flotilla of cargo I was. . . no water-wings to inflate.   Imagine those wings

I did not have   but suspected were present   when it was calm enough
to reflect and pull faces into focus.   Wishing is like sadness at sea.

Say, you are on a beach with waves—the circular myth of family collapsing.
I had this part-time job of being a daughter apart—job that paid in tips

for those with damp inward pauses.   Deep water girl
who keeps washing up anywhere.   Everywhere.

I was a surprise to those gathered in bed.   How I rose to float in
on a man and woman dancing in bed.   Or were they clouds?

I could not keep them straight   (though they were trying
hard to act happy)   like knives flying simultaneously as birds

at twilight.

The Sea

owns bastions of death

Windy Miranda on the beach gauges storms for Shakespeare—

theirs   the island where Prospero magically loves her   Father

present at the beginning   Newly born man—

before augmentation

iii. *reliquary*

Mentor Thinks Along with Telemachus

. . . if that's what you want . . . initiations by air
anywhere near the water   No other contacts

(The waxy moon will stick by me over the Aegean)

Wax moonlike then and full   Waves fill
Questions do arise   You'll grow heavy   waiting

for answers

(Perpetual   my lost son sounds   From me
freshly frozen in sunlight   lips bitter   Feel how that hurts?)

Make your breathing palpable   There   Now slower

(Am I but a small animal relying on dirt   wind and water?)

Note the threshing floor: the butcher floor: ocean floor: love
made on a bed   Mammals   in the brown autumn leaves

(Would it help to make myself more evident   and heard on the floor
of some quaint Senate   Bossing around those without history

Me, acting like that?)

One life at a time   Please   go for the part
known implicitly—sudden green clearing of birds without entrails

They still inform you

(Who spoke for me   saying, *Blabber you must.*
Battle with things of size, and all you find minisculely beautiful.)

Wise people slept their way to recovery in long-ago caves
    Finally at home with themselves in the dark
        No need to talk anymore

Addiction

Can one really stand straight in the sand—
a posture diminished by war
and abandonment

Telemachus has no idea what coils beneath
the waves

Fixations   Mirage   Or strange men
that just might make a father

From the beach   boy watches radiance
swell to a god like no other

Day by day and at dark   Telemachus bends
to the wet cloak of his own body

Question wears him thin   Thought wore him crooked

Embryonic Sons and Daughters,

You are the flexible ones who are warned and have time still
to find home.
           Remember your inward doze for forty unblemished
weeks when you never cried for mother.

Minute gold energies flicker in rocky streams. Mountain-time ticks. Pacific
marks itself with howling hot hours.   Overviews bring in the ocean,
or in reverse the high-plateaus might indicate *foresight*—if only we can allow
the wind free passage from west to east.

A broken line of anything shows where the hopes are buried.

I paddled the Humboldt searching for magical fishtails to fashion
into condor wings—that elevation, one to lift me up and off
the coast of Chile.

But back to you, friend Telemachus—and the future of these
nearly-perfected humans.
           Each misstep recalls how crookedness
can begin and end a story.

And to think that not so long ago we were bound to killing, fire in the woods,
and meat from a fresh hunt oozing . . . but then the hardest lesson—
how to care for another.

Ever wish we were otherwise occupied, simply born with the button
for wisdom in place? In mind? Not that one lackluster question:
okay, so it's never the real future anyway?

Perhaps it's our own fearsome slide backwards to relax *en utero*
until we're good and ready to get born.   *What say you*
large or tiny ones?   *Talk.*   *Now.*

               No matter, it's you
who'll make the difference, if indeed there is a difference to be made. So take

one big breath and dive inside that great (up you go) wave building until you see through our human-clown charade. From Earth's hot core and out past icy Neptune, we're suspected of being the laughable and unwise species.

Tiny Gills

Feel slits in your neck pulse with oxygen
bubbling through.

So much swirling you think you spot in the attic
corner a goat carved at the foot of a three-eyed
shepherd on the sarcophagus—final resting place

for the god of planning. You sigh, loosening
oceans of air stored since childhood.

Strange   that Penelope

does not question or pray in a selfish manner
Nor is she a narcissist with fanciful selves
startling from her mirror

But at times (not known to many) Telemachus watches
her levitate at sundown   for she too is out looking

He searches through her eyes until they form a long line
of clouds   Never complete

(Maybe she too would have asked for more
had she known the power of speaking)

Say   in the middle of one half-truth another comes bottoms-up
from a Bog of Ink that throws up broken phrases
but never finishes a sentence

Can anyone stop *yes*   from shifting   full-force into   *No*
dopey kid   you alone did not cause the split in your parents
It's a dilemma arriving way before you

Pithy little essay (this one)   and fixes rarely swoop
from a wilderness of choices

                              Elemental puzzles of fire
earth   and wind over water   add profundity to puddles
of ignorance

That loopy number eight counted too in my murky ball
as a child   Closed track of infinity   Over and over
the same route
               No better way to learn than with friends
and enemies who swap places   but can't change
who they are

Mother I Could Be

The truth of fools (and of toys too) should be wise:
Flashes of no-nonsense slurs about the future
embedded with *likelihoods and   possibilities*
at times   never.

(I shook that childish Eight Ball hard too.)   Thumped it
so it could make sense.   Tell me one true story. Mine
might be the Best.

I thought about that a lot, and worried.

Predicaments were dire—much squandered back then
as now.

Time now to check over your shoulder, little beach boy. You, my mythic son
of a Great Greek he-man. Islander.   Sailor and outlier.

As I said, *Look at your back on the beach. It is me, and if it weren't*
for the land-masses and clocks between—you could have been mine,

or maybe me.

Reliquary

He handed her the iconic mask in a parking lot, and the nearest
trunk flew open to waves of light on an inland sea.

Byzantium brushed peacocks into dying pines, and low gold
bees moved from bud to blossom   as the young do.

A gong struck. Streets went dark with *sanskara*—fists
in every garden.
                                    Phases of time that knew where to drop
down hard. Signs of waste, of laying waste.

With that in mind, she pressed a finger to the cool one's temple
then down her cheek, saying,
                        Sling silver arrows, and charge my clouded mind
with what eternity can do.   At night a hand unscrewed her head
and sprinkled pollen on the heart.

My Good Man

Anything   not to be in a door that slams at will—
who cares for the legs   heart and head
in a speechless family

The fact is that the feet move [and face] forward   and owners
learn to count

I count each night   Three hundred sixty-two
excursions add up   to *death of mind in an Asian marsh*

War does what it does
                              to hold us further apart

What of that other man I dreamt with his feet on backwards
Our eyes steady   shut at length   Ankles jammed
in at bad angles are not a sign of companionship

Who is it   I kept trying to try on   then throw off

I do not move at daybreak (neither do my eyes) until the third
of June   His death-day over again   I fly loose and deep:

          Hello my good man   who took to war like anything human
You   the child caretaker of church ashes and altar   You with the father
who sold onions and deer from a truck
                              Patriarch that mopped the county
asylum floors at night for more money   Not around much
but anciently blamed for the distances he kept

Refusal

Photo of an iris recalls the missing petal—pressed to a glow. It's an energy that won't

succumb to circumstance. The twilight of what left, rising and eerily real. No future like

that of the fresh survivor and no past like that of a relic—dead pheasant shoveled from

the road, but for one wing prone and blowing in my headlights. Another refusal to leave

at once, and go quietly.

Oh My Gods, and Those with Salt Haloes

on the Aegean, we're no longer conscious and have babies
of our own to outgrow.

Boom loud enough for those lost on land.

Filled with denial we sit (and have sat) on our hands
finding that pose comforting until we begin to appear
admirable to others and so many looked to us for help.

Aren't we as capable of extinction as any of the
cow-gobbling hoards.

Huge crashes tend to make us jump, then creep
to the water closet.

Indecision is not a path toward improvement.

And what of our formidably blocked imaginations—
white spaces and silence that drives us nuts. Without
wonder no curiosity. And vice-versa

Who can find a gavel big enough to beat brains into
the naysayers: The Not-me-ers hahaha-ing/ and LOL-ing
ones of muffled words.

Gray curls inside my skull, a labyrinth some think we've
mastered: *Mister Man.   Ms. Brash Upstart.   Madam of
Provocative Syllables.*

As anyone on the go, I flip the finger at the thought
it might be me who tracked shit across our freshly-watered

planet.

Of Space

Dear deep mirror, Come double for what once was brave
and without greed or sly gold winks.   Give us discernment
enough to take the red road slowly.

What say you, my wayward glass   so filled with story?
You hold the crack through which spirits trickle
back in spring.

April, wide open and unborn . . . how the years catch me
wanting still   for I live on slippery ground
between rivers of clay and rain on the ocean.

Ready to dissemble   the promise-words tossed out?
Sway I will with algae and the wandering fish fed up
with human sediment.

But there go the remnants of my blue silk scarf   swimming
through an epic melt of ice.

Glacial :   that which   loosely translates into diminishment
(quite haltingly acknowledged).   Our need to own
huge chunks of water.   Oxymorons loomingly big.

Who stamped ice with a brain of sorts anyway?   Bit in the mouth.
Poor cold being flagged to death by humans.   Colorful flags
a sure sign of *Mine (not yours, you selfish grunt).*

Then the power of *Who got here first in a boat (feet first*
or last in the sand)?   Semaphores wave furiously at the future.

Who said   vision counts?   Materials to discount.
On sale—those pickled pink feet with the naked fore
and hindquarters.

Numeric proportions suggest extending large to Huge
and the sequential nature of one two three never will
connect to *ad infinitum* anyhow.

Fake simplicity you think(?), Mr. Whatever you are,   no matter how crazy
you bumble about.   Hey you, face up, and count to one hundred backwards
in the same breath.   Now stay there.   Hard of hearing?
Is it hard to hear of other than yourself?

Look way up there where the name still is   **night sky—**

Field of cosmic blinking.   The unalloyed and jeweled
in black holes.   Our ringed planets.

                    The opulence of space.

The Interstate Chimera

i. young omens

The overpass children out for the day as happy
as hand-painted bundles of wool that slip from the east.

Caught in traffic, I imagine each child the pleasure of disowning
its name.
        One shape, and in a line, is a skewed way to think
of children—small constellations we've locked inside our story.
Who wants to be a perfect young omen, or even that prospect?

Such guesswork while the antique hour of noon floats above
my motionless car.
           Birds perch on a chimney. Little girls and boys
walk by the hand of one taller and thicker than them. No rules set
rigidly on these faces during a cloudless span of time.

How to align the distant blue mountains with a truckload of shit
and caged chickens idling beside me?
           How to creep past our stalled,
flummoxed world—I recall one long-ago Sunday, when awed by Joseph's
coat of fuzzy colors something turns fishy—Joseph grins. I watch him in
his story as if he were one of god's smirky angels. Above the rest is he.
Even his nose points up. You know the way little girls track love
in a favored doll's eyes—before *good*   *better*   *best-loved*
flips to *not you anymore.*

ii. brother-rage

Why does a boy in his new coat arouse such madness in a brother?
Splashes of biblical goat blood   More to that gift than fleece corded,
boiled, and dyed.   Father pushes hard love
on one son.   Joseph.   See the way that he's smiling?

Coiled brain of *brother-rage* ignites. (Is there a more familial line of hatred?)
No simple envy once *the* frenetic-mind takes hold.

iii. *sky flock*

Now here comes a different desert arching and falling into stretches of sand.
Bells clunk in the man's head: this shepherd who spends nights under stars
over his flock
                        wants much more for his sons—and turns to root-longing.
Possibilities he shuts up together by the fire, and more keep coming:
until by dawn imagination fades like a bell. Slowly it goes quiet.
Quits.   Quite misunderstood, that way of seeing
falls to pieces.

iv. *migrant mind*

Another might-have-been tale sprawls through the long migration
(had only our shepherd known more about writing much more)—
if only he'd written

A guide the stars are to this sky-minded shepherd   who dreams north
for his two boys, one so like his mother. Both he leads from the desert.
As cold wind   they flow and fly from cloud to cloud (not to be confused
with an afterward life). *What mighty Boys . . .*
thinks their father to his sheep (exalted frame of communion)

as his offspring lift away from all that went before.

[Footnote: dreams   sons   or the sheep   what does this man
want most not to lose?]

v. *glasses of whiskey*

The overpass kids gather above   (and a bit before) me   Unmothered
and fatherless this chimera of children—cluster of arms with almost a single head
bobbing over the Interstate   my own private blend   Creature songs (swell)

those I used to know

                    Overtaken   I am by these mountains   On the car seat
beside me   raw turquoise the shaman traded for glasses of whiskey in the cold
Andes

         This stone in traffic has me release the hand of a child—one after another
Belled sheep   clink in the pastures   Scarlet-flagged   these years
and miles from nowhere   Each

a floating presence at noon

iv. finding time

The Right Frequency

allows the next stillness to occur. Welcome each space
as it appears but confirm slowly—

                        as if an adage drifting
down through centuries of smoke.

Try a later roll in summer grass with its sundial fingers
holding you on top the seven-veiled mysteries
of green.

Above that, motionless clouds predict it's never lickety-split
to the apparent state that counts.
                        Urn, goat, and crimson altar-cloth
are flighty suggestions, hard to pin down despite humans
and their sharpened articles of faith.

Tie a select few to the calf-bell of dogma, then with due respect
leave the dotted lines.

Maybe even get off your mount (the high one) and walk beside
those roped or chained, and stumbling.

Each time you are kind, feel how your breath changes,
the frequency of birds at dusk settling in.

Be aware.   One pivotal moment
      does not foreshadow a calmer forever on earth.

Jewel

After dreaming of the coastal range all night,
I wake to an elevation uncomplicated

by words—
            the notion that we shall meet again
I wanted you to know so hold out space

like a watered jewel

The silent work behind each tidal pool and peak
along the ocean.

Of Water Made

Ever make bets on who lives best inside
their mother's womb?

Don't forget from that question.   Drag *en utero*
your spine around and forward face the eloquence
and mindlessness of man.

Made of water, we are tagged with sudden glints
of drowning.

Favor eyes above the waves,
                              that kind of vision.

It's why the eyes keep score—flotillas of us out there
aimlessly looking.

Who's to make it home?

Telemachus thought about this a long time,
long ago by the sea.

Street of the Three Sad Marias

Let's you and I sail off, Telemachus, for the coast of Chile.
Old sailors pointed at storms from the crow's nest—winds high,
clouds purpling—out of control energies looming overtime.

Like family.

Today there's a lack of good swaddling cloth on the world market,
and overdose seems the most affective cure for the present.

Check lately on your family of origin,
or was it of choice?

Could this be our last chance to breathe in a temperate zone
as you gallop the shore, then rest your pony under nine-foot fern—
stretches of beach to rough-ride as you grow wild with air.

Throw pinches salt over your shoulder (and do ask for wisdom)
as you see the long line of glass buildings
tower to the north.

Here the condor rides altitudes of mountains.   Fins flash
as lighting blows up the coast, and one unfathomable waterspout
skids from the sea to roar through pricey shops on *Via de las tres
Marias Tristes.*
                    Pray to the Holy Trinity or the raw power
of barometric pressure dropping   then find yourself a bar
on the beach with the parrot that speaks seven languages
and laughs in, and at, most.

Kingdom

There could have been time for another life before the strong March wind
swept us from us from all-fours, and dropped us near the water.
Mirrors waiting.

No denying that the Nth degree of the unknown is upon us, and there's no hint
of direction for our wasted planet. Our run at flamboyantly hot lifestyles shrunk
the ice (and more) to pieces. Huff and strut, and we've about destroyed
the globe.

We mark time, belch, and remain on the lookout for chatter, though truth is
we are most awkward within the family circle where the food tastes good
but the term *lineage* shows ugly signs of meltdown.
                                        Who sits where
at the last family feast (?) when any mention of disagreement is met
with angular glares of *Thou shalt not repeat tales of personal or climate crisis.*
And thou shalt instead sip all thy wine then nod at the endlessly grinning?

My determined place at that annual folly? I doze with my clutch of poems
in the family broom-closet—me, yet another calculated risk to the authenticity
of family history.
                Cursing in couplets, tweeting of human drift measured in masses:
poor continental wanderers—lost infants, men and women. The elders choking on
water, while in my pine-oiled burrow I grow heavy and sniff broom straw—one
way back to the lost animal kingdom.

Argus

Remnant fur of time   Dog asleep

Smoke trailing from the bald fields

Great hollow animal horn
        filled with late October   Cornucopia

Autumn's store

Dog   the breathing sigh of plenty

Earth divided, reseeded into a plan   to be taken
seriously

Fertility shades in with ash and rain

Telemachus wonders what on earth
will be his sonic guide   The sea washes in   then out
an anguish of his own making

Night   brings the howl of old friend Argus
He   who loves beyond blindness

Later in time   and by the Sea of Japan
Basho filled with grief
writes tersely

skull in the grasses/what remains of a soldier's plan

Most airy
silk worm
drops down
through days
that escaped

counting
Through mixes
of sun wind
and water
Worm attached
to the floating unknowns
of a mulberry leaf
Basho comes to himself
late in a field near the sea—
the unplanned planted beneath
his grassy feet

Clocks

mark time with watery bells
for what has happened
is done

Couples in seaside parks walk about
with the sonic buds poking from
their ears—blankness worn firmly
as the common face of man

Tiers of demolished eardrums for the teens,
muffled infants howl in blues or pink
never knowing the world
left behind

Fire excites   Book-talk turns
nasty   Politics sicken   Garbage
offers a place to sleep in the dumpster
Decay   Combustible compost
Tire smoke

How did we get to this particulate and toxic
place where little makes a difference

So what   if we flee in this direction or
stand still by the water

Breathe in the ocean   Choke on brainwashed
filth   Separate   we think we are   wildly disorganized
and sniffing our planetary loom

In front of us   (if you can see that far)   a faded sun
slips down on the horizon. Time for the invisible
to clock-in

Sewn to the Skin

Who's to soften this boy's fury?

History such as his is the story of
a twilit mother who extinguishes time

or is put out by another.

children know who left for another.

Who wants to sleep beside a father
or mother anyway?

Bedtime   the old construct for missing each other—
late at night when the thoughts come flying,
and the mind won't sleep,
and the sheep don't work.

Lament of two who once shared a bed.
Love is made of lamb-side softness
felt one to the next.
                        Touch sewn to the skin
is a child's longing.   Belonging.

Dream of one's kind.   Boy-man
child-father.   The mother-daughter pairs.

They're family   to the living

Starfish Wash-Up

and they too are goners. The water birds losing
feathers—blue and gray, they stand on one leg
in marsh-stench near the ocean.

Up and down
the beach.
and for as far as I can see is trouble,
as again this year hobbles giant deep-sea mother.
She's lost her turtle eggs and cannot go one more
heave in the sand.

My baby girl, you who definitely has it in those level blue eyes,
hang on and don't let go in mid-catastrophe.

Once a lighthouse cast brightness in my hometown. Tattered red flags
signaled old human precognition but only for the dead. Parts of porches
and window frames likely represent the same flotilla of the damned
that passed this way last year.

And always, that creepy lane of cars (or people) searching for any
road upland, sideways, or northward—just not to meet their end
at a standstill.

Storms get wider and bigger by the season, closer now
to standards that thrilled Prospero and Miranda.

Infant child, I cover your small face with my fingers so you'll remember
best my hands that swaddle you in muslin.

The strongest of cottons.

For wasn't it you with me in our watery life years ago in Chile?
Sailing.   Dreaming, I found you whole—pearl
of a skull and watery eyes filled with the salt wind.

—for Celine

Finding Time

A son is born to many women.   Mothers love beaches
and the child who walks them.

The beginning of June or the future was not declared
happy or sad   beforehand.

There's a slowness to the hills when the tide comes in
    meaning the boy inside a man waits before he goes.
        Love embodies then turns aside.

Every look at the Aegean   Telemachus stops to ask more.

Fathers coming home from war lose track of things like that.

Odysseus finds time to gather his son and the sand
in his arms,   or not.

overflow of an unknown self: a song of songs

D. M. Spitzer

Sara—in gratitude, in friendship, in admiration
for "a love made rich and supple by the makers' hands"

Canto 1.

I am a mouth
opening   closing

full of your mouth's
kisses

sweetest wine
overflows
the mouth the tongue   the breast
                                        speaks your name drains

                                                                    phial after phial
                                                                    of honeyed air & voice

behind you   youth   gasps   desire   unsheathes you

                                                                    chases you
                                                    and your fragrant whispers

                        let us draw ourselves towards another in reverence

            let delight   enclose us

                                                into a chamber of treasures
                        opening   where the mysteries
                            deliver another self of selves

you are a name and you are names untold
the breast speaks a river
of wine follows
the curves of your self over-
flowing self

Voices and names
the breast speaks dark
body
dark as shadows
beneath a host of cedars

daughters of the holy city
look away

I am a sun
draped in the riches of blackness   longings   sun-
blackened
are brothers at war
within me

they station me
at the vineyard's gate

I do not guard the vineyard
I tear down the vineyard's walls

secrets lead my breath

to you   where poems range

beyond city walls
where the sun at its highest moment
covers you in sleep

isolated
embracing
beneath the midday sun

depart   from awareness

along   footprints
                                              of poetry

into   its tabernacle of dusk

you   overflow   all
                                                                                          likeness

                                                                          face of doves in the season
                                                                          of ripeness

                                                                          neck a cove embracing smooth
                                                                          water in its curve

                                                                          an image of gold touched with silver

incense wreathes the pharaoh's chamber

everything   leaning back   on something else

           bound together   chest

                                on my   chest

                                laid low among the courtyard's shadows

clusters of copper gleam in the vineyard

                                        you overflow my mouth
                                        eyes the magic of bright doves in sun-filled air
                                        ripening in my glances

                                        our bed
                                        all the world's shadows

           beneath   limbs   of dark cedar & cypress

Canto 2.

I

flower
of the plain

lily   of deep   hollows

you

lily
between   uncurling
             leaves

and blossoms   overflowing   all
                                                               others, boughs
                                                               heavy with fruit
                                                               in a wilderness

                                                        a garden

                                        a paradise of our flowering selves

deep the shadows

               longing for you I

                      stretch out on the cool floor

                              full of the fruit of your mouth

               on lips

               tongues my throat full of your sweetness

               mouths

               raise a call

send me under a roof of wine

gasps arrayed opening mouth

open upon me

crowd   the overripe, the lush, the orchard's

                   fruit deepening in sweetness

                                    I am an open mouth
                                    of longing an omen   a hand
                                    under my head another
                                    slips around my waist

daughters of the holy city   away

        I scribe the boundary line
        through powers and forces
        of the dust-filled wilderness

                awake   awake   out
                                                of selves

                mouths agape at our desire

                stay   far

far   a voice   out of my own voice
                                                a lost brother
                                                in the eye of wonder

                leaps and draws near
                out of distant mountains
                bridging the divided world

                    grace-tipped hooves
                    clatter on bare
                    stone landed
                    from the far range

desire
                    behind a wall a closed gate a hand poised to strike
                    tangled in a hunter's net

the voice   unwinds itself   from coiled silence

                                                    overflow me
                                                        beauty filling me over

                                                    a dove out of reach

        a storm of hailstone   torrent overflows sky a body of numberless shadows

earth flowers a new beginning
time for severing blossom
from stalk
closes as a tomb
full

                             our paradise
                     the dove-song
                     ripens in our ears

                     the fig between our lips
                     breaks the winter

        the grape-clusters shine copper   sweeten the air

                                              overflows beauty selves and bodies
                                  spills on shoulders thighs hips the sacred dove
                                                  in our mouths' kisses

the sacred dove sheltered among the stones of the garden wall

gaze from   your eyes
song from   your mouth

all time is pleasure is a pair
of sleek foxes
vanished
made rich with fruit

clusters blaze copper throughout the vineyard
where they roam and feast without end

tend   the poem
& its legend   along banks of lilies   until day exhales

shadows fill themselves
with the light's closing body
set themselves in motion   towards night

turn   grace-tipped hooves
                                clatter on bare
                                stone landed
                                from the far range

the mountains lift   ravines to the wealth of night

&   sink   themselves   to   hollows

Canto 3.

I sought you   upon our bed   in the night

the soul   a mouth opening a kiss
                                          breathes you in the night closes
                                                   full of you

and I seek you and I do not find you and I call your name and I am unheard insurrections, breaths

      I draw my own image

              in circles around the whole city longing
                   for you pulls me out of self is a ring
                    traced on the marketplace
          a circumference on the open plaza
                breaking the circle of myself edged
                        on its own edge without—

        I seek and time future cages me
                in loss and I do not find you

                   I am a stone plunged
               in the plaza's fountain wave
             circles empty of you finding
          only myself prisoner of my own

             desire circles my footsteps
        draw over the cityscape
     breath opens
  a mouth bereft of your

names your mouth's kisses

I will close the circle turns me I return longing turns

and the chamber of riches seals itself behind our embrace

daughters of the holy city away
I scribe the boundary line
through powers and forces
of the dust-filled wilderness

                    awake   awake

mouths agape at our   desire   is distance is
                                           an unknown self
                                           risen from the desert
                                           a pillar of smoke
                                           offerings frankincense
                                           and myrrh

the bed of Solomon
        a whole city an army
                crowned with scimitars

        a field of battle

        a man
        a sabre at his thigh
                all of night's wonders
                dazzling in his eyes

in the night I will find you the bed
the bed of a king gold and silver posts
a canopy stained with the secrets of the murex

daughters of the holy city
gasp to see love crowns the shadow past the limits of the un-
known self love a dynasty passing as a day reaches towards night
and another day of wisdom & splendor on the bodied pulse of an-
other self

Canto 4.

night overflows song overflows voice

behold   you are beauty

eyes   the magic of bright doves in sun-filled air

a tapestry of songs
from before the waters
withdrew from the earth's back

your mouth
full of an unclothed
darkness trimmed
with rouge

voice   the rise and fall of seasons
ripen bring to fullness disrobe
all of earth's wonders

silence
is the face
of god

quiet as stone
ripe
full of secrets

as the jeweled seeds overflow the pomegranate

the tower of David encircled
by fire ten thousand
stone gates and spears of bronze

a bare neck towers

into night

                                    the day exhales
                        its shadows I will journey past myself
                        to the holy mountain beyond the sea

          beauty

                    a terminus
                    overflows me

desire pressed upon desire is freedom of freedom's way away
in its mouth its own end its breath   away its lion-set enclosure
                    its panther-shrieking mountains

hearts from the rising falling breast
are eyes are gasps pass moist lips   the throat sings

                                        courses your figure
                                    curves along yourself
                                a river of wine
                            we slake each other
                    mouths tongues   breasts

from your lips wine flows
                        to my mouth
                        your mouth is honey milk from your tongue mixes on your mouth's
                        kisses   I drink   I swallow

                    opens
         a secret garden
                   a garden closed
                   a spring overflowing itself
                   an orchard of   fruit-
                   bowed trees

a sacred spring at the middle of all we do an unknown source blooms & overflows us

                   partake of the garden
                   eat of the fruits of my mouth

         feast   of the unknown self a paradise

                   down to the floor knees to the gravel paths
                   bodies gathered to the fruit-covered earth

Canto 5.

enter the unclosed garden

harvest the fruit of my mouth
I am bread for your hunger
I am milk on your lips
I am wine dark as sun-blackened longings & all of night's riches

I lie   I fall
sleep does not touch
the lover's heart   a voice
a lost brother calling out the wilderness

run your hands along the gate at the garden's edge   where I am always awake

enter the garden

unclose me

overflow me   the holy bird the flight to another self

                                    the sleeping face touched with dew
                              overflowing the primal waters and darkest night

                                                disrobes me

how cover self that is no self but you another self withdraws from the open
        hand the hollow cry the written word as body yearns

                        uprising
                        against the word
                        unclosesquake of hands   unclose selves

                from your mouth a breath
                you and not you

I am seeking you   my own voice   trauma on my face

and I do not find you   turns me to myself   and a speaking mouth

I call your name   lost from you found   tears from me

I am unheard   in the cycle of speech   veil of selves veil of selves

confounds—

from the mouth's wall of speech a company of charging warriors
takes away the other self that is no self

awake   daughters of the holy city
awake   I scribe the boundary line
                through powers and forces
                  of the dust-filled wilderness

      a mouth gapes

                                   lost shorn
                                   brother

                        word in ruins countless
                            unfilled wants

I am seeking you   unlost

crown of gold   silver pine risen to the stars   hunger raven-black

omen on the lips

                the surface of rising waters
                doves white as sea-foam
                the sun-filled air
                infinity
                        a blaze on the sun-splashed
                                flooding waters

a silent tide pools
in the basin of your neck
your mouth's words
before any words a breath
sweetens the air across lips
shed sacred names as petals as
breath overflow the mouth

                                        in low-relief your hands
                                        blossom the light the earth

        a box of ivory inlaid with lapis
        a forest of columns marble white as doves
        upon a foundation of dark gold

        an image of smoking incense

        wrap the tall cedar posts
                        inside our sanctuary   honey
                        the voice all desire

daughters of the holy city
wake

Canto 6.

lost brother

in a wilderness of beginnings

a gaze   turned away

seek   together   the expired

love   a   down-going
into gardens of the underworld

phantoms gust the dark valley
                gather lilies on its endless slope

I   a down-going

                        beauty overflows
            the way things seem   breaches the riverbank

                        of self

as

                        the holy city
                                declines within its own seasons

as

                        a marshalled host
                                raises dust
                                into the blood-streaked twilight

love   is terror

                            an imminent assault
                            on all you feel

turn   your eyes   look   away

          eyes as doves
          startled
          into flight

a tapestry sways on the fortress tower full of songs from before
the waters withdrew from the earth's back

songs overflowing themselves

your mouth   full of unclothed radiance
                          trimmed with sunrise

                          the rise and fall of seasons ripening and bringing to fullness

                          silent as the voices of god riven in stone a quiet face full of secrets
                          as   the mystic pomegranate shimmering with seeds

in the desert of numberless
                          faces each a grain of sand

                                        your face a dove of god
                                        casting shadows
                                        over the whole landscape

                        gazes and blessings overflow untold mouths
                        speechless in their wonders their uncertainties

                                        what is this love
                                           a dawn
                        splicing earth and sky

                        a crescent moon
                drawn on a shoulder
                                                bare in moonlight

                                        a sun
                proclaiming the way
                                                of all desire

                                                an armored host
                gleaming like the stars   banners raised and striking awe

see genesis
a storm
inside the walnut grove

see blossoms
strung on vines and tendrils
reach and reach for the light

          the rivers blossoming in flood

       breasts risen   in exaltation
        in the noise of delight of wonder

on banks of self & self chariots on the horizon thunder down to oblivion

Canto 7.

love

turn

return

      a gaze enfolds us in its eye

      white dove blazing in twilight

      gaze enfold in an eye yourself turns

          a ring of dancers in the eye of the threshing floor

            in the eye of an invading army

            bivouacked

            around the pulsing

            heart

footsteps cross the stone floor   blossom   in my ear
                                    the rhythm of thigh and thigh

                as

                                            oars skimming the sea's wine dark skin

                as

                                            my hands over your unclothed thighs

the eye

      a force in high relief

            arriving after everything seen
            in its time of flowering

valley of lilies
slopes along the shadows of   your   waist your neck   a tower of ivory

            half   in shadow

eyes   are   mountain lakes
                      untold   unfathomed

                      a thousand gates and night-watchmen surround
                      what you see

                      a thousand faces launched in each breath
                      steered by another eye
                      one face turning fore and aft

love

        cloaked
            an emperor in robes
            of twilight

                       how many hours escape us
                         what pleasures hide
                         in a love made rich
                         and supple
                             by the makers' hands

dates ripen and fill
the walled garden

pass   between our mouths

                                                    each mouth   quenches and thirsts
                                                                              for the other

            say   *I will climb the palm tree*
                                    at the garden's edge
                                    I will be made strong
                                    among the wind-touched leaves
                                    at the highest places

            say   *I will be fruit for your mouth*
                                    and the wine crossing
                                    again and again
                                    over your parted lips

I fall   you rise
from   from self
self I rise   you fall

                    come love

                    let us go out to the field
                    let us play music in the scattered villages
                    let us wake at dawn among the broad leaves of the vineyards
                    let us see the vineyard bloom copper and full of passion

  and

                                        the rivers blossoming in flood

        there   there   I will open myself
                                                 pressed to you

                                   breasts
                                                 as tides beneath quiet starlight
                                                 the garden's fragrance
                                                 in sheets around our naked selves

all the orchard's folded limbs as doors opening around us

I watch the glistening
dew before the sun
ornament the ancient ways

Canto 8.

to return
with you

to a single source
to be united
in the rising breast of another

I found you
            beyond the limits of self

where

I am a mouth
opening
closing
full of
your mouth's
kisses

sending me through and beyond oblivion

time not yet
embraces me
as my arms close around you

presses me leads me
enters me

.

and

        I take your wrist
        through the narrow passage
        return as to the source

            to the chamber of riches within our embrace

   what is not yet
   drains us

       as

          I drink you the wine streaming

                    from your mouth

                    speaks a name
                    a blessing
                    hovers around
                    my head

                    full of the wine

        your hand
        beneath my head another hand
        slips around my waist

daughters of the holy city

                                          away

                       I scribe the boundary lines
                           through powers and forces
                           in the dust-filled wilderness

awake   awake

                          out of selves

mouths agape at our desire

                         stay   far

who   is this   approaching
clothed in white blossoms
escorted by a lost brother

out of the dark hollows of memory

              beneath the tree   heavy with fruit
                              I wake you

                              the center of all
                              beginnings

the fruit tree ripe at the garden's center

                              I

                                   a jewel a secret closing opening
                                   the codex of your heart's sanctuary
                                   the scrolls of your heart's caverns

love is as mighty as death
full of unseen
full of unknown

                                    stretching into a time without
                                                time
                                                as
                                                the song sweeps you
                                                into itself
                                                as
                                                the hunger
                                                for what is concealed
                                                that moves
                                                heaven and earth
                                                spreading itself
                                                on wings of awe
                                                and reverence

                wings of flame

fire shapes the flow of time

given unto the fire a self burns to ash to naught but fire itself enters the lover's gasping breast

into each day

fire turns to poem
scribed as legend written
from ashes
in the book of eternal longing

if a wall rises
into the field of love
we shall make it an abode
build upon its ridge
a parapet of silver

       if love forms a gate
       we shall write ourselves
       upon its surface
       we shall be the cedar of its making

I am a wall

            I am a fortress with spires
                within your gaze

as

           you   are   my   freedom

in Bethlehem   far

                        an orchard grew
                        in the name of Solomon
                        given to the watchers
                        the lovers
                        the guardians
                        of the sacred bond

                                                take up the fruit
                                mouths opening
                        closing

become   silver basins   full

                                                    of love's unending song

a garden   of selves
                                            bare
                                        and face   to   face

                numberless   mouths closing
                                                                    unclosing

                                                                    full of the kisses
                                                                of their lovers' mouths

lay me down in the dawn-swept garden
wet grass beneath my back

our voices
woven into one song

hear yourself beyond self
in the breath of another

let it pass

                                                          let it pass

                                              fire breaking over a river of fire

            swift in the garden   swift and bright
            conflagration over the burning mountains
            blaze aromatic in sheets around the ecstasy

            the delight of overflowing
                          our naked unknown selves

Notes

Love tells you to care for the people on the edge of the light
—David Bowie and Queen[1]

I. Notes on the Text

This translation is based on the *Septuagint* (LXX) text edited by Rahlfs and Hanhart,[2] with occasional reference to the Latin Vulgate, John Wycliffe's 14th century middle-English translation project (JWV),[3] Martin Luther's 16th century German translation, and the 17th century King James English translation (KJV).[4] The term *Septuagint* here refers to the translation into Greek of Jewish scriptures. It may be that the *Song of Songs* was translated into Greek in a period after the translation of the Pentateuch, the Five Books of Moses. Indeed, as some have suggested, the composition or compilation of the *Song of Songs* may have taken place during the same period as the *Septuagint* in its narrower sense—the translation of the Pentateuch, which is to say, around the 3rd century BCE.[5] In the broader sense of this great translation project the *Song* then found a place, a translation into Greek: Treat has suggested a date of translation in the range of the 1st century BCE-1st century CE.[6] Other sources enriched the project in other ways—notably, Chana and Ariel Bloch's translation from Hebrew and their introductory essay on their project and some of the scholarship collected in Athalya Brenner's volume *A Feminist Companion to the Song of Songs*[7] and the second series, co-edited by Carole Fontaine.[8]

The *Septuagint* (ca. 3rd century BCE) takes its name from the legend of its production. To Alexandria were summoned six members from the twelve tribes for the purpose of a translation into

---

1 "Under Pressure," by David Bowie and Queen, track 11 on Queen, *Hot Space*, EMI, 1982.

2 Alfred Rahlfs and Robert Hanhart, eds., *Septuaginta*, 2nd ed. (Stuttgart: Deutsche Bibelgesellschaft, 2006).

3 References to the JWV are to the text presented in John Wycliffe, Frederic Madden, and Josiah Forshall, *The Holy Bible, Containing the Old And New Testaments: With the Apocryphal Books, In the Earliest English Versions*, vol. 3 (Oxford: Oxford University Press, 1850), 73-84, HathiTrust, https://babel.hathitrust.org/cgi/pt?id=chi.19477504&view=1up&seq=81. Hereafter this text will be cited with chapter and verse followed by a page reference, e.g. (JWV 1:1; p. 73).

4 Throughout this essay the abbreviations given for these translations will be used when citing passages.

5 Chana Bloch and Ariel Bloch, "In the Garden of Delights," introduction to *The Song of Songs: the world's first great love poem*, trans. Chana Bloch and Ariel Bloch (New York: Random House/The Modern Library, 1995), 24-25.

6 Jay C. Treat, "To the Reader of Song of Songs," in Pietersma, Albert, Wright, Benjamin G., and Wright, Benjamin G., III, eds. *A New English Translation of the Septuagint: And the Other Greek Translations Traditionally Included under That Title* (Cary: Oxford University Press, 2007), 659, ProQuest Ebook Central.

7 Athalya Brenner, ed. *Feminist Companion to the Song of Songs* (Sheffield: Sheffield Academic Press, 1993), ProQuest Ebook Central.

8 Athalya Brenner and Carole Fontaine, eds., *A Feminist Companion to the Song of Songs*, 2nd Series (Sheffield: Sheffield Academic Press, 2000), ProQuest Ebook Central.

Greek of Hebrew sacred writings. One form of the legend narrates that the scholars' versions were identical: "God gave counsel to the heart of each one, and they all agreed as one mind."[9] Eventually the name *Septuagint* (seventy)—rounded down from the seventy-two scholars—arose to describe the text created on that occasion.

Whatever underlying texts enabled the ancient translation from Hebrew into Greek are now extremely fragmentary: the Dead Sea Scrolls (1st-century BCE-2nd century CE) preserve some texts in varying degrees of material soundness, but the *Song* does not appear intact in the scrolls.[10] One encounters then the curious situation that, in a material sense, the translation precedes the original. Or, if that sounds too hyperbolic: the *Song* exists primarily as translation.[11] Something akin to this may account for the composition of the *Song*, as well, for the text may present a compilation or anthology of *songs* that undergo unification in their critical-interpretive reception.[12] In formatting *overflow of an unknown self* I have created separate, numbered sections and called them "Cantos," gesturing both to the Latin title (*Canticles* or *Canticum Canticorum*) of the *Song* and to its condition as *both* a unity *and* a multiplicity, a gathering, an arrangement of flourishes, an anthology—which I take to be one valence of the compelling title. Even though the numbering ordains a sequence, the anthology might be fruitfully read in other and various orders; I hope the numbers do not interfere with such readings.

II. Trans-figuration

Of the principles guiding this work, the main attempts to unsettle interpretive traditions by making thoroughly unconventional choices throughout the text and to craft a work of contemporary literature in English. Whether or not *overflow of an unknown self: a song of songs* finds a place within your ideas of what constitutes translation, it decidedly, heavily leans on the indefinite article *a* in its subtitle. That monographic, monosyllabic indicator might be compared to a hyphen in *trans-lation*; let it punctuate and activate a spacing on the site of expected categories, not fully delinked from them yet likewise not fully embedded within them.

Because the translational practice at work in *overflow of an unknown self* differs from and exceeds translation, the term *trans-figuration* might be a useful supplement, substitution, or embellishment. One feature of this practice emerges in the approach to repetition. While in *A Heaven Wrought of*

---

9 "Babylonian Talmud Megillah 9a-b: Translation of the Torah into Greek," trans. S. Berrin, in *Texts and Traditions: A Source Reader for the Study of Second Temple and Rabbinic Judaism*, ed. Lawrence H. Schiffman (Hoboken, New Jersey: KTAV Publishing House, 1998), 218. Aristeas reports in his famous epistle a somewhat different scene involving consultation among the seventy-two that results nevertheless in a complete translation in seventy-two days that is as if "achieved by some deliberate design." So agreeable is the translation that the seventy-two insist that it should remain static, that is, without revision. "Letter of Aristeas," trans. R. J. H. Shutt, in *Texts and Traditions*, 211-18.

10 Exum gives a good summary of the remains of the *Song* in the Dead Sea Scrolls. J. Cheryl Exum, *Song of Songs: A Commentary* (Louisville: Presbyterian Publishing Corporation, 2005), 28, ProQuest Ebook Central.

11 See Debel's persuasive article, in which he argues for the inclusion of (at least some) ancient translations within the concept and study of the "dynamic process of the organic growth of the scriptural texts." Hans Debel, "Greek 'Variant Literary Editions' to the Hebrew Bible?," *Journal for the Study of Judaism in the Persian, Hellenistic, and Roman Period* 41, no. 2 (2010): 190, JSTOR, http://www.jstor.org/stable/24670889.

12 That an assumption of some type of unity underlies various interpretations of the *Song* is Schoenfeld's thesis. Devorah Schoenfeld, "One Song or Many: The Unity of the Song of Songs in Jewish and Christian Exegesis," *Hebrew Studies* 61 (2020): 123-142. doi:10.1353/hbr.2020.0019.

Iron: Poems from the Odyssey (Etruscan, 2016) I translated the "formulaic," recurring phrase δύσετό τ'ἠέλιος σκιόωντό τε πᾶσαι ἀγυιαί (e.g. *Od.* 2.388) in a variety of ways in an attempt to let resonate the improvisatory oral character of the poem, I have translated some recurring phrases in the LXX text of the *Song* in a way that repeats without variation. Among these is the address to (or of?) the "Daughters of Jerusalem," repeated through four of the eight Cantos: "daughters of the holy city away / I scribe the boundary line / through powers and forces /of the dust-filled wilderness" (Canto 2, p. 145; 3, p. 154; 5, p. 168; 8, p. 191).[13] In repetition of this sort I am reaching for the lost music of the *Song of Songs* and offering a reminder of choruses sung in performance. Another aspect of this striving takes the form of 'white-space' throughout the Cantos, where I hope to have cleared an area into which readers' imaginations might project their own 'music' or elaborations of the poems' images or something else.

The variation of repetition only echoes in the wide variance from other translations. One example of this repetition and variation across and through other translations sounds in Canto 2:

> grace-tipped hooves
>> clatter on bare
>> stone landed
>> from the far range (Canto 2, pp. 146, 149)

The KJV translation gives:

> My beloved is like a roc or a young
> hart (KJV 2:9)

and then:

> be thou like a roe or a young hart upon the mountains of Be'ther (KJV 2:17)

Through a play of synecdoche ("grace-tipped hooves" for "roe or a young hart") and metonym ("bare stone" and "range" for "mountains") the phrase evokes through resemblance something of the KJV repetition *and* that in the LXX text, which has its own internal variations.[14]

At some moments within the text of *overflow of an unknown self* the language seems to collide with the LXX language of *Song of Songs*, ricocheting from translational impact with the text's imagery to chart parting trajectories. The discussion above of the phrase "grace-tipped hooves" helps to illustrate this aspect of trans-figuration. More radically, the final Canto follows—or rather, develops—smoldering pathways illuminated by the passing fire imagery in the LXX *Song* (8:6),[15]

---

13 LXX 2:7; 3:5; 5:8; 8:4. Treat has heard in this recurring phrase an "implied polytheism" that LXX "does little to tone down." Treat, "To the Reader of Song of Songs," 658.

14 τῇ δορκάδι / ἢ νεβρῷ ἐλάφων ἐπὶ τὰ ὄρη Βαιθηλ (LXX 2:9); τῷ δόρκωνι ἢ νεβρῷ ἐλάφων / ἐπὶ ὄρη κοιλωμάτων (LXX 2:17).

15 περίπτερα αὐτῆς περίπτερα πυρός, φλόγες αὐτῆς (LXX 8:6); "the coals thereof [sc. jealousy] *are* coals of fire, *which hath* a most vehement flame" (KJV 8:6; my interpolation).

reworking the fire image from a single verse in the LXX into a theme coursing from the phrase "wings of flame" through to "fire turns to poem / scribed as legend written / from ashes / in the book of eternal longing" (Canto 8, p. 195). Yet, other moments translate a phrase in a familiar way, as in "love is as mighty as death" (Canto 8, p. 193).[16]

Some places work to alter an image sufficiently to render it more inclusive than it might otherwise resonate (see the discussion below for more on this). In Canto 2, for example, the image of "his sweet fruit in my throat" (ἐν λάρυγγί μου [LXX 2:3]), which seems to be a fairly transparent reference to fellatio, has undergone a transformation, altering the location of the fruit and focalizing the mouth rather than the throat[17]:

I

stretch out on the cool floor

full of the fruit of your mouth (Canto 2, p. 144).

The KJV translates the line as "his fruit was sweet to my taste" (KJV 2:3), but the JWV translators write "his fruyt *was* swete to my throte" (JWV 2:3; p. 74). Even as another verse of the *Song's* second chapter may present an image of cunnilingus (2:16),[18] distributing pleasures of oral sex among the lovers, I have translated in this way so as to widen the image. Reorienting it away from a more specific range of sexual practice(s) I have translated in the direction of a broader, hopefully more inclusive image while preserving the *Song's* focus on the mouth and face: the images of this section of *overflow of an unknow self* pass through lips, tongues, and even throat. (Canto 2, p. 144).

In other places trans-figuration involves the practice of formulating a poetry that folds into itself the language about language: elsewhere I have described this and termed it a "meta-language poetry."[19] The beginning of Canto 8, for example, does something similar in rendering the future tense of the verbs in the LXX text as the grammatical subject of the lines with the phrase "time not yet" (as in future):

time not yet

embraces me
as my arms close around you

presses me leads me
enters me (Canto 8, p. 189).

---

16 Compare "for love *is* strong as death" (KJV 8:6); and "for strong is as deth loouc" and "for loue is strong as deth" (JWV 8:6; p. 83).

17 As Exum has put it, the "lovers' faces are animate focal points of the body." Exum, *Song of Songs: A Commentary*, 21.

18 At least on Case's reading of the Hebrew text and comparisons to several other ancient texts. M. L. Case, "Cunning Linguists: Oral Sex in the Song of Songs," *Vetus Testamentum* 67, no. 2 (2017): 171-86, JSTOR, http://www.jstor.org/stable/44647550.

19 D. M. Spitzer, "Translator's Note, B. Lyric," in "Displacements: Poems of Trauma & Migration from Ancient Greek," *Ancient Exchanges* 1, no. 1 (2020), https://exchanges.uiowa.edu/ancient/issues/departures/displacements/.

Still another aspect of trans-figuration as it unfurls in *overflow of an unknown self* attempts to generate aural features of the Greek version of the *Song* within the English poem. An example of this dimension of trans-figuration can be heard in some of the opening lines of Canto 1:

> phial after phial
> of honeyed air & voice (p. 137)

Repeating the aspiration in *phial* draws on the repetition of these sounds where the LXX translates the first speaker's exhortation of | for another's kisses with the phrase Φιλησάτω με ἀπὸ φιλημάτων (*philesato me apo philematon* [LXX 1:2]). A more oblique instance resounds in the first phrase, where "I am" attempts to echo into the English the work's title in its old Greek translation (Ἆισμα; *Aisma*; song).

III. Towards a *trans-* of trans-lation

overflow of an unknown self composes a *Song of Songs* for the trans-moment. In the LXX translation of the *Song* pronouns, adjectives, participles all indicate gender.[20] The *Song's* opening line illustrates this, where the possessive pronoun αὐτοῦ (*autou*, his) genders as masculine the mouth from which kisses flow:

> Φιλησήτω με ἀπὸ φιλημάτων στόματος αὐτοῦ (LXX 1:2)
> *osculator me osculo oris sui* (Vulgate 1:1)
> Kisse he me with the cos of his mowth (JWV 1:1; p. 73)[21]
> *ER küsse mich mit dem Kusse seines Mundes* (Martin Luther's version 1:2)[22]
> Let him kiss me with the kisses of his mouth (KJV 1:2)

Of these, only the Vulgate version leaves room for possibilities beyond a feminine speaker calling for kisses from a mouth of a masculine lover, though by 1:4 the adjective *nigra* genders the first-person speaker.

Revealingly, the *Codex Sinaiticus* (around 350 CE), one of the earliest manuscripts of the (relatively) intact and complete Greek Bibles, adds red-lettered script centered on the page that identifies the speaker(s) in each scene: the opening lines quoted above, for instance, follow a rubricked ΗΝΥΜΦΗ, the *nymphe*, the bride. In that ancient text no ambiguity is allowed to play in the line summoning kisses, redoubling the gendering of the song. Similarly, in the JWV translation

---

20 Though, as Treat has observed, there remains some ambiguity in terms of gender that "can make it difficult to follow a dialogue." Treat, "To the Reader of Song of Songs," 661.

21 In the text available to me, one column of the Wycliffe version marks each speech with a statement identifying the speaker; here, the identification is "The Chirche, of the comyng of Crist spekith, seiende." Wycliffe, Madden, and Forshall, *The Holy Bible, Containing the Old And New Testaments*, 73, HathiTrust.

22 The text of Martin Luther's translation is from https://www.bibel-online.net/buch/luther_1545_letzte_hand/hohelied/1/#1, accessed 29 July, 2021.

a heading above the first chapter reads "Heer gynneth the booc that is clepid Songus of Songis, of the bridalis of Crist and of the Chirche," while a note in the margin on the opening page states: "In this book the spouse is God; the spousesse is hooli chirche."[23]

One result of this gendering of the sensual loving that unfolds in the poem is to contain the *Song* within a circle of heteronormativity.[24] Yet, if it is true that, as the Blochs have written in the introduction to their translation of the *Song*, according to the *Song's* "abundance and generosity" "a lily is a lily is a woman's body is a man's lips is a field of desire,"[25] might this abundance be extended by a 21ˢᵗ century translation to unfold the love celebrated in the *Song* into a similarly plentiful network of possible relations *beyond* a man-woman | male-female paradigm? As the poetry of *overflow of an unknown self* formed itself through an extended period of trans-lation | trans-figuration done in 2012 through to editing in 2018 (when the manuscript was first sent to Etruscan for review) and re-editing in 2021 (when Etruscan developed the present *Tribus* volume), the heteronormative circle became increasingly frayed and, hopefully, broken at least enough so as to let in a bit more light,[26] a little more of the multi-formed, multi-colored, and expanding spectrum called love, at least until the one name refracts into many names.

IV. Queering

Throughout *overflow of an unknown self* reverberates a practice of Queer Translation along lines articulated by Jon D. Jaramillo in the Queer Translation Collective's *Manifesto*, insofar as *overflow* both "emphasizes bodies" and "rejects the binary use of gendered pronouns that erases same sex desire."[27] The gendered English pronouns "he" and "she" and their variants and possessives ("his" "her") are only used in this sentence, nowhere appearing in the text of *overflow of an unknown self*. By actively working to eliminate the gendering of the Song's principal speakers, narrators, agents, *a song of songs*—again: emphasis falls on the use of an indefinite article (*a*) rather than the definite article (*the*)—becomes possible as a location wherein the prismatic spread of LesbianGayBisexualTransQueerInterAsexual+(expansiveabundance) might find openings for a love unbound by the gendered pronouns and the consequent determinations of heteronormativity. Aspects of the *Song's* rich imagery suggest the opening of a trans-gender field, where certain images remain in play as they describe now this, now that loving body in the text.[28] If this work of literary

---

23 Wycliffe, Madden, and Forshall, *The Holy Bible, Containing the Old And New Testaments*, 73, HathiTrust.

24 As Brenner has written, the Song addresses "heterosexual love and its erotic manifestations." Athalya Brenner, "On Feminist Criticism of the Song of Songs," in Brenner, *Feminist Companion to the Song of Songs*, 28. On James' reading, the city-scape itself is also gendered, but in a manner that reconfigures, complexifies, and ambiguates what she identifies as a broader Near Eastern motif associating the feminine and a beleaguered or threatened city atypical of love poetry. Elaine James, "Battle of the Sexes: Gender and the City in the Song of Songs," *Journal for the Study of the Old Testament* 42, no. 1 (September 2017): 93–116, https://doi.org/10.1177/0309089216670546.

25 Chana Bloch and Ariel Bloch, "In the Garden of Delights," 32.

26 Paraphrasing Leonard Cohen's lyric: "There is a crack in everything, that's how the light gets in." "Anthem," by Leonard Cohen, track 5 on *The Future*, Columbia Records, 1992. Lyrics from the transcript on https://www.leonardcohenfiles.com/album10.html, accessed 21 May, 2021.

27 Jon D. Jaramillo, "Manifesto," https://queertranslationcollective.org/manifesto/, accessed 21 May, 2021.

28 Carol Meyers, "Gender Imagery in the Song of Songs," *Hebrew Annual Review* 10 (1986): 212, http://hdl.handle.net/1811/58719 (reprinted in Brenner, *Feminist Companion to the Song of Songs*, 200).

art, sometimes considered the most beautiful love poem of all time, has become more inclusive at last through the trans-lation | trans-figuration called *overflow of an unknown self*, it is long overdue; let this be a beginning in the direction(s) of the myriadic overflow of loves, desires, intimacies, sexes.

The "I," "me," and "you" cross, or find the threshold(s) of singularity, the boundaries of grammatical number. As grammatically both singular and plural "you" bears its own crossings and never releases the tensions of self-selves. Such tensions do not resound as oppositions, they are not "problematic," but instead are encoded into address, including self-address in the form of reflection and reflexivity: the 'you' of self-dialogue, as a moment of the 'you' of address, takes place as the dynamics of plurality inside a (dream of) singularity. Though the "I" and "me" are grammatically singular, the poem in which they are spoken regularly pushes them to (and beyond?) limits, as the singular self finds itself breaching its own edges, overflowing into an "unknown self," reconfigured, relayed into more diverse moments through the trans-porting, trans-forming powers of loving relations. A passage early in the opening canto revels in this movement, in the mysteries of a "we" wondrously emerging from the fullness and overflow of mouths, kisses, voices, breaths:

let us draw ourselves towards another in reverence

let delight   enclose us

into a chamber of treasures

opening   where the mysteries

deliver another self of selves (Canto 1, p. 138).

If there lingers any voice of an allegorical-theological reading of the Biblical *Song of Songs* it resonates in passages where the singular finds itself always-already a plural, a plurality of erotically charged, bodied loving.

In its three appearances within *overflow* the divinity called "god" in the poem always comes to language as an embodied image reflecting the human lover(s), returning like an echo back to and beyond the speaker's | speakers' self | selves. Thus the poem sings

- a "face of god" (Canto 4, p. 157) and "voices of god" (Canto 6, p. 176), both of which fill to overflowing the lover's | lovers' face(s) and voice(s) with the resonant calls of secrets, hewn *as image* wrought by human beings (the faces of god are said to be stone),
- a "dove of god" (Canto 6, p. 176) that, in its full expression names the lover's | lovers' face(s): "your face a dove of god."

In short, the divine of *overflow* always names and (re-)figures the human and, more specifically, the loving *human bodies* celebrated in the song.

Does such a queering translation enact an interpretative violence on the text? Yes, to be sure: to make a song from the *Song*, I have shattered the text and then arrayed the shards for a new configuration, one that does not say at the outset "Love = 1 man + 1 woman," and one whose images generate further and other images. Many other, readily available translations exist of this work and are not in the least threatened by this one. Furthermore, the violence perpetrated here does not differ in kind (though perhaps by degree) from other modes of interpretation, each of which will involve shearing, straining, or reshaping aspects of the *Song* according to its own interpretive principles or framework. In his survey of the ways Christian exegetes have engaged the *Song of Songs*, Stephen Moore has illustrated how 'allegorical' readings (broadly construed) reconfigure the basic "enabling assumption" of non-allegorical interpretations—namely, "the mutual attraction between a male and a female"—into something "still more unthinkable" to late ancient and Medieval Christian readers: "an erotically charged relationship between two *male* parties."[29] The *Song of Songs*—this song or anthology of songs announced in advance as a kind of pinnacle or at least a *primus inter pares*—arrives to contemporary audiences as already having been queered.

Let this translation widen the reach of that task, hopefully inviting more and more numerous arrangements of loving bodies to find a celebration of an ever-expanding horizon of sexualities radiant with the bright, multicolored lights and possibilities of inclusion.

Let this translation be suggestive to other translators who might continue that celebratory task, for *overflow of an unknown self* too is but one further moment in the *Song's* becoming through the mutually enhancing, transformative work of interpretation and translation. If lights always form a boundary, let us run to the edges or just beyond into the richness of darkness, summoned by love's exhortation "to care for the people on the edge of the light."

---

29 Stephen D. Moore, "The Song of Songs in the History of Sexuality," *Church History* 69, no. 2 (2000): 331-32, JSTOR, doi:10.2307/3169583.

Acknowledgments

Ann Pedone

Thank you to the following publications that published earlier versions of these poems: *Howling Press*, *Blazing Stadium*, *Blaze Vox*, *Hole in the Head*, and *West Trade Review*.

Katherine Soniat

Many thanks to the editors of following journals for first publishing the following poems:

Artemis: "Mentor Thinks along with Telemachus," "Sewn to the Skin, " "Street of the Three Sad Marias"
Asheville Poetry Review. "Refusal," "Argus"
Five Points: "Finding Time," "Telemachus Seeking," "Penelope's Womb"
Fulcrum: Missing," "At Large"
Hotel Amerika: "The Sea," "First Nature, Once Removed," "The Interstate Chimera"
ONE: "Starfish Wash-Up," "Of Water Made"
The Opiate: "Losing Touch," "Embryonic Sons and Daughters"
Pedestal: "Orphan Joy"
Permafrost: "Agua"
Plume: "after birth"
Shining Rock: "Half Life"
The Thinking Republic: "Mother I Could Be," "Tiny Gills," "Scream"
Tiferet: "Jewel," "Before the Looking Glass," "Island," "Of Space"
Xavier Review: "Telemachus Pondering the Bottomlands," "That Morning I Saw Telemachus"

D. M. Spitzer

Before everything else, I thank Sara Shiva Spitzer for over twenty years of love "made rich and supple by the makers' hands" without which this project would never have been developed.

In terms of reflecting on the process of translation, I would like to acknowledge the Queer Translation Collective's manifesto produced by Jon D. Jaramillo, available at https://queertranslationcollective. org/manifesto/. Through a reading of this manifesto I gained insights on how the translation was already queering the text and how, with slightly modifications, I might make it even more inclusive. Furthermore, Stephen D. Moore's "The Song of Songs in the History of Sexuality" in *Church*

History (69, no. 2 [2000]: 328-49) illuminated ways in which the *Song* has already been queered throughout its reception history.

Resources in the volume *Feminist Companion to the Song of Songs* (Sheffield: Sheffield Academic Press, 1993), edited by Athalya Brenner, and the second version she co-edited with Carole Fontaine (2000), helped me gain perspectives towards an understanding of the text when reflecting on it for the "Notes" section. Towards a working view of how and when the text may have been composed and then translated into ancient Greek, I have appreciated the scholarship of Jay Treat in the expansive *A New English Translation of the Septuagint: And the Other Greek Translations Traditionally Included under That Title*, edited by Albert Pietersma, Benjamin G. Wright, and Benjamin G. Wright III (Cary: Oxford University Press, 2007).

Finally, with the Blochs' translation (New York: Random House/The Modern Library, 1995) as a guide when teaching the *Song* in a course called "The Bible as Literature" during the fall, 2016 term at Binghamton University, I engaged in critical dialogue on the poem and its meanings. For this I would also extend thanks to the students who took part in that course and to the Departments of Comparative Literature and Judaic Studies for the opportunity to conduct that class.

About The Authors

Ann Pedone

Ann is the author of *The Italian Professor's Wife* (2022, Press 53), as well as the chapbooks *The Bird Happened, perhaps there is a sky we don't know: a re-imagining of sappho, Everywhere You Put Your Mouth, Sea [break]*, and *DREAM/WORK*. Her work has recently appeared in *The American Journal of Poetry, Chicago Quarterly Review, The Louisville Review*, and *New York Quarterly*. She has been nominated for Best of the Net, and has appeared as Best American Poetry's "Pick of the Week."

Katherine Soniat

Katherine Soniat's life has moved around a lot in the last few years: trying hard to find the RIGHT HOME, and why not be most concerned about our planet EARTH? *Starfish Washup* will be her ninth collection of poetry, to be published in Spring, 2023. *The Swing Girl* (LSU Press, 2011), *Bright Stranger* (LSU Press). *Polishing the Glass Storm* will be available through Louisiana State University Press in fall, 2022. *The Goodbye Animals* won the Turtle Island Chapbook Award (2014). She has been on the faculty at Hollins University and Virginia Tech, and has taught in the Great Smokies Writing Program at UNC/Asheville. Her poetry has appeared in *Hotel Amerika, Poetry, Iowa Review, The Nation, Women's Review of Books*, and *Superstition Review*, among others.

D. M. Spitzer

Author of *A Heaven Wrought of Iron: Poems from the Odyssey* (Etruscan 2016), *abyss of departures*, an image|text collaboration with digital artist Sara Shiva Spitzer (Hawai'i Review, 2020), and editor of the volumes *Studies in Ancient Greek Philosophy in Honor of Professor Anthony Preus* (Routledge, 2023) *Philosophy's Treason: Studies in Philosophy and Translation* (Vernon Press, 2020), and with Paulo Oliveira *Transfiction and Bordering Approaches to Theorizing Translation: Essays in Dialogue with the Work of Rosemary Arrojo* (Routledge, 2022/23), D. M. Spitzer is a scholar, poet, and translator focused on early Greek thinking. Spitzer's work has appeared or is forthcoming in journals such as *Research in Phenomenology, Epoché, Diacritics, Ancient Philosophy*, while his poetry and translations have been published in *Ancient Exchanges, The Maine Review, North American Review*, and elsewhere. Currently, Dr. Spitzer is writing a book on the ways migration and trauma shaped the thinking of the earliest Greek philosophers, as well as working on a translation of only the similes from the ancient Greek epic *The Iliad*.

Also By

Ann Pedone

The Italian Professor's Wife
The Bird Happened
perhaps there is a sky we don't know: a re-imagining of sappho
DREAM/WORK
Everywhere You Put Your Mouth

Katherine Soniat

Starfish Wash-up
Polishing the Glass Storm
Bright Stranger
A Raft, A Boat, A Bridge
The Swing Girl
Alluvial
A Shared Life
Cracking Eggs
Notes of Departure

D. M. Spitzer

A Heaven Wrought of Iron: Poems from the Odyssey (2016)
abyss of departures, an image | text collaboration with digital artist Sara Shiva Spitzer (2020)
Philosophy's Treason: Studies in Philosophy and Translation, editor and organizer (2020)
Studies in Ancient Greek Philosophy in Honor of Professor Anthony Preus (Routledge, 2023), editor and organizer
Transfiction and Bordering Approaches to Theorizing Translation: Essays in Dialogue with the Work of Rosemary Arrojo (Routledge, 2022/23), editor and organizer with Paulo Oliveira

Books from Etruscan Press

The Candle: Poems of Our 20th Century Holocausts | William Heyen

The Confessions of Doc Williams & Other Poems | William Heyen

The Football Corporations | William Heyen

A Poetics of Hiroshima | William Heyen

September 11, 2001: American Writers Respond | Edited by William Heyen

Shoah Train | William Heyen

American Anger: An Evidentiary | H. L. Hix

As Easy As Lying | H. L. Hix

As Much As, If Not More Than | H. L. Hix

Chromatic | H. L. Hix

Demonstrategy: Poetry, For and Against | H. L. Hix

First Fire, Then Birds | H. L. Hix

God Bless | H. L. Hix

I'm Here to Learn to Dream in Your Language | H. L. Hix

Incident Light | H. L. Hix

Legible Heavens | H. L. Hix

Lines of Inquiry | H. L. Hix

Rain Inscription | H. L. Hix

Shadows of Houses | H. L. Hix

Wild and Whirling Words: A Poetic Conversation | Moderated by H. L. Hix

All the Difference | Patricia Horvath

Art Into Life | Frederick R. Karl

Free Concert: New and Selected Poems | Milton Kessler

Who's Afraid of Helen of Troy: An Essay on Love | David Lazar

Mailer's Last Days: New and Selected Literary Remembrances | J. Michael Lennon

Parallel Lives | Michael Lind

The Burning House | Paul Lisicky

Museum of Stones | Lynn Lurie

Quick Kills | Lynn Lurie

Synergos | Roberto Manzano

The Gambler's Nephew | Jack Matthews

The Subtle Bodies | James McCorkle

An Archaeology of Yearning | Bruce Mills

Arcadia Road: A Trilogy | Thorpe Moeckel

Venison | Thorpe Moeckel

So Late, So Soon | Carol Moldaw

The Widening | Carol Moldaw

Clay and Star: Selected Poems of Liliana Ursu | Translated by Mihaela Moscaliuc

Cannot Stay: Essays on Travel | Kevin Oderman

White Vespa | Kevin Oderman

Etruscan Press Is Proud of Support Received From

Wilkes University

Youngstown State University

The Ohio Arts Council

Community of Literary Magazines and Presses

[clmp]

The Stephen & Jeryl Oristaglio Foundation

The National Endowment for the Arts

The Thendara Foundation

Founded in 2001 with a generous grant from the Oristaglio Foundation, Etruscan Press is a nonprofit cooperative of poets and writers working to produce and promote books that nurture the dialogue among genres, achieve a distinctive voice, and reshape the literary and cultural histories of which we are a part.

etruscan press

www.etruscanpress.org

Etruscan Press books may be ordered from

Consortium Book Sales and Distribution

800.283.3572

www.cbsd.com

Etruscan Press is a 501(c)(3) nonprofit organization.
Contributions to Etruscan Press are tax deductible
as allowed under applicable law.
For more information, a prospectus,
or to order one of our titles,
contact us at books@etruscanpress.org.